Chris and Joy

June, 1973

George

BONEFISHING

OTHER BOOKS BY STANLEY M. BABSON

Diversions in a Busy Life

Where Sands Are Pink

BONEFISHING

STANLEY M. BABSON

WINCHESTER PRESS

Drawings by G. Don Ray and Matthew Kalmenoff

Photographs on pp. 22, 26, 30, 46, 67, 69, 70 by Molly
Adams; 44, courtesy Bahamas Information Serv-
ices; 49, by Donald Wiedenmayer; 77, courtesy
Bahama Ministry of Tourism; 79, 83, 84, courtesy
Bahama News Bureau; 86, 90, 91, by Hy Peskin.

Library of Congress Catalog Card Number: 72-96088
ISBN 0-87691-092-4

Published by Winchester Press
460 Park Avenue, New York 10022

Printed in the United States of America

Contents

Thanks and appreciation—

TO STANLEY M. BABSON, JR., for needling me into writing this book, and to his wife, AMELIA O. BABSON, for her help with the art work.

TO MOLLY ADAMS, photographer, and DON MC-CARTHY of the Bahamas Development Board for their photographs and permission to use them.

TO DR. LAVETT SMITH, MRS. PHYLLIS CAHN, and RICHARD LUND, all of the American Museum of Natural History in New York City, for their help in constructing the chapter on the bonefish life cycle.

TO THE ZOOLOGICAL SOCIETY OF NEW YORK for the use of Miss Gloria Hollister's article on bonefish larvae.

TO DR. DONALD S. ERDMAN of San Juan, Puerto Rico, for the use of his studies on the eating habits of bonefish.

TO DONALD E. MORRIS, aquatic biologist of Hawaii, and the New York State Conservation Department for their help on marine lore.

And finally to LEE WULFF, DANA LAMB, FRANCIS HATCH, SAM SNEAD, JOE BROOKS—anglers supreme—for their various contributions to the script.

S. M. B.

Foreword
by Lee Wulff

Back in 1947 when the first bonefish were taken on a fly, we who flyfished the flats for them knew that a fish with a hitherto modest reputation would soon move into the front ranks of the world's most respected game fish.

Previously the bonefish had been recognized for its wariness and for its speed when hooked. The fish was guaranteed to be sporting on three-six tackle (rod 6 feet or over—tip under 6 ounces—and 6-

thread linen line, 18-pound test). And sporting it was, even though the fish had to lug an ounce of sinker along with it on its runs.

The accepted belief was that the bonefish would not have any interest in a fly or lure because of the angle of its mouth and its method of feeding. A bonefish was caught by casting well ahead of it with a live shrimp or other bait. To cast anything near it was to scare it half out of its wits. We all believed this then—or at least half believed it. This was before we developed spinning gear that doesn't require lead weights and before the first of us had made serious attempts to present a fly near the "ghost of the flats." Until then the ounce of lead that made the cast possible landed with quite a splash, and it was no wonder the bonefish was spooked.

How bright is this new star in the sport-fish firmament? Time will tell, we thought twenty-five years ago when the publicity started. And, slowly but surely, the bonefish has taken a solid position near the top of the sporting list.

The bonefish does not jump like a tarpon or a salmon, and those who have grown used to leaping fish may miss this attribute. But then, neither does a brook trout leap, and nor do brown trout very often. The bonefish doesn't fight the river's current, and it doesn't demand so delicate a fly as does the trout. True, there are no mayfly hatches on the bonefish flats, and that special world which is so identified with trout and obliquely with the Atlantic salmon will remain peculiarly their own.

Compare a bonefish and a freshwater bass. The bass may jump, but when it comes to speed and power the freshwater fish is left far behind. To catch a bass, 35 yards of line is adequate; for a bonefish an angler feels naked with less than 200 yards.

The bonefish has its own world, and it is a good one. When the salmon rivers and trout streams are bearing coats of ice and their devotees can play the game only by tying flies while they talk of next spring's conquests, bonefishermen are catching fish. It is a sport that's like the sea in which this ancient fish swims, open to everyone and available at all seasons.

The "fox of the flats" is like the best of the freshwater fish, a quarry that can be sought out, hooked and played, and released by a single individual or an angler with a guide. The bonefisherman can wade if he wishes, or fish from a small boat. He can fish with a fly, with an artifical lure, or with bait. He is sure to be foiled again and again by the fish's wariness, its selectivity, or even its wisdom, for bonefish are released and caught again and again as trout are in the "fishing for fun only" streams.

The bonefish's world is a most beautiful one—clear water—shallows in the sunlight where the tides rise over the light-colored sands—a world where a bonefish needs speed to outdistance a predator. The predator, be he a barracuda or a man, needs patience and skill of his own.

As fewer and fewer of the bonefish caught are kept—and to maintain the quality of the fishing, fish must be released—more and more of the fish swimming the flats will be old veterans. As the sport grows, progressively more skill will be required to bring bonefish to the fly or lure.

Time will favor bonefishing if anglers continue to release their fish. Though we may lose our trout streams and salmon rivers to dams, logging, industry, and other manifestations of expanding civilization, most of the sunlit flats where the bonefish swim should stay fresh, clean, lonely, and inviting to the angler for generations to come.

Stanley Babson, with sensitive judgment, gives the bonefish its due, and with this, the first book on the bonefish, he opens for any who care to enter a new arena of suspense and pleasure.

Lee Wulff

Hooked by
the Bonefish

It all started in Canada when I was five or six years old, at a family place on the St. Lawrence River. There was a boathouse, and I used to lie on my stomach and fish for sunnies and yellow perch in the clear and sparkling water. For bait I used worms dug from the garden in back of the kitchen, bits of salt pork, or sometimes minnows discarded by older anglers at the end of a day's fishing. I was not allowed to have a knife at that age, but it didn't matter. I found my teeth an adequate substitute in cutting bait of the proper size to fit the pin which served as my fishhook.

I spent many hours this way, but my love of fishing was not really rewarded until the day an enormous bass swallowed at one gulp my hook, line, and sinker. I could not lift him from the water, so I yelled for help. My wails of distress finally reached my family, who came running to rescue what they no doubt felt was a drowning offspring. When they dis-

covered what the uproar was about, my father, a man of action, seized a nearby net and with one swoop brought in my first bass, a 3½-pound smallmouth. My place was secured that moment, and the next day my father presented me with a rod and reel.

That was a long time ago.

Since then, I have fished throughout the world and have run the gamut of fishing in salt and fresh waters —from sailfish and tarpon of the ocean to salmon and trout of river and stream.

Thirty-odd years ago I found the wily bonefish— *Albula vulpes,* white fox of the sea, and, to my way of thinking, the king of them all.

And it has been a kind of survival of the fittest, for while I love all kinds of fishing and am thrilled to feel the play of any fish at the other end of a taut line, I have found that for many reasons bonefishing gives me the greatest thrill of all.

There are countless books on deep-water fishing, fishing for bass, salmon, and trout, but for some reason there has been no book on bonefish. The great writers of fishing literature—Zane Grey, Edward R. Hewitt, Ray Bergman, Kip Farrington, Van Campen Heilner, Roderick Haig-Brown, Joe Brooks and Lee Wulff, for example—have written abundantly of salmon and trout, of marlin, sailfish, tarpon, and the rest; and while chapters and articles have appeared from time to time on bonefish, this is the first book.

There are reasons for this. Until thirty years ago bonefish were not considered sport fish. They were thought to be strong fighters but were fished mostly by natives with handlines or netted. Today bonefish are not only accepted as a sporting fish of the highest order, but impressive tributes are being paid to them by leading sportsmen. Van Campen Heilner told me that though he has fished all his life for everything from the brook trout to swordfish he regards the bonefish as king, and in his experience the gamest fish that swims. If there were a piscatorial hall of fame he would put a bonefish in the center on a pedestal all its own.

Our great fishing President, Herbert Hoover, said of bonefish, in *Fishing for Fun,* "You have to hunt for them and where you find signs of where they are, you cast them a shrimp. At times they will be digging for a hermit crab. Then they will put their tails out of the water and wag them at you. Most times they are not eating shrimp that day. Other days the water is too cold or the tide runs out or the bonefish just stayed home." And with dry humor Mr. Hoover adds,

"This is good practice in restrained thinking."

But there may be another reason why bonefish have been slow to attain social equality with salmon and tarpon in the literary world. No fish has been more hotly debated, and perhaps no writer has been sufficiently brash to take a position on something about which opinions differ so widely. Take any group of assorted fishermen, and if you want to start an argument, just make a few comments like these: "Bonefish are greatly overrated as sportfish." "Bonefish pound for pound will outfight any fish that swims in either fresh or salt water." "Bonefish are not fit to eat—only good for marlin bait!"

I believe *Albula vulpes* has stirred up more controversy in recent years than any other sport fish, with the possible exception of the Atlantic salmon. Just why this tantalizing, unpredictable, unorthodox, and amazing fish should have had such a devastating effect on countless anglers, both mentally and financially, has posed a question I have been trying to answer for a long time.

Hunting and fishing are the second and third oldest professions, yet bonefishing is the only sport I know of, except perhaps swordfishing, that combines hunting and fishing. I know of no more thrilling sight than a school of bonefish feeding over a white flat with their tails shimmering in the sunlight while the hunter stalks his quarry in order to get a cast at them. Stalking feeding bonefish requires patience, stamina, and judgment in getting into the proper casting position without making the slightest noise. I have seen an experienced angler shake with buck fever while stalking a big tailing bonefish, and even expert casters can botch the job in the excitement of this new sport.

The well-known fly fisherman Dana S. Lamb described his first experience in an article in the bulletin of the Anglers' Club of New York some years ago. He was on a Florida flat with a 4⅛-ounce Payne rod and a 9-foot leader tied to an Edson tiger fly:

Almost immediately a pair of feeding bonefish appeared. "There they are," my guide Keith whispered with ill-suppressed excitement. Nervously I drew line from my chunky Arnold reel and got it out with false casts. About to drop the red-and-white streamer in the path of the cutting fin I was dissuaded by Keith's warning that I was casting to a shark. Then I saw the bonefish, silver-gray fins and sickle tails cruising along the bank in quest of buried marine fauna, sending up little clouds of mud from the bottom. I have taken salmon upwards of 30 pounds and more than once cast fairly calmly to very substantial trout but now I definitely had buck fever. My knees knocked together, the calves of my legs turned to jelly, and the loose bottom boards on which I stood rattled alarmingly. Summoning all my willpower I cast, kneeling as I did so. They saw the fly. Two tails were lowered, two fins cut the water in pursuit. For a foot, 2 feet, 10 feet they followed. Then, catching sight of the boat, they boiled in two swift turns, and two ridges in the water indicated their precipitous retreat. Limp as a rag I collapsed and attempted with palsied hands to light a cigarette.

Joe Brooks, one of the world's finest fishermen, told me in a letter (April 15, 1964) about his first encounter with *Albula vulpes:*

The first time I saw a bonefish slipping quietly along in ten inches of water, I fell for him. This was at Peterson Key, out from Islamorada; guiding me was famous Captain Jimmy Albright. The time was June 1947. I had been invited to the Keys by Allen Corson, then outdoor editor of the *Miami Herald.* With me was Nelson Edwards, Paramount Newsreel cameraman, and we were making a movie of Florida fishing.

I asked Jimmy what chance I had of taking a bonefish on a fly.

"There are records of four men taking bonefish on flies," he said. "In each case they were trying for other fish. They thought that catching the bonefish was an accident and didn't try for them again. But I think you could catch them on a fly."

"There's one now," he said, "straight ahead, tailing."

I saw the fish, its tail waggling in the sun as he dug in the bottom of the shallow water. I made a couple of false casts and dropped the fly 2 feet in front of his nose. He charged and as I brought the fly back in slow, foot-long jerks, he followed right in back of it for a couple of feet. I kept stripping. Then he took. I struck, and that fish took off with unbelievable speed, a silvery ghost racing pell mell across the flat, like nothing I'd ever seen. My salmon fishing experience paid off. I kept the rod high, let the drag keep him from getting a slack line. When he hit a channel the line went down, and suddenly there he was rushing across the shallow flat on the other side. He stopped after an over-all flight of some 600 feet. I began to breathe again, laid back on the rod, turned him and got him coming. He followed along, getting his breath, as I reeled fast. He came docilely until he saw the boat, then he bolted. I weathered that storm and now he was 150 feet away and this time I brought him back to within 40 feet of the skiff. He began to circle, and round and round he went. Finally I held the rod tip up, got his head high and reeled him in, kept him coming over the net Jimmy was holding. And there he was. He went about 8 pounds.

Bonefish
Characteristics

Bonefish are found in tropical waters and warm seas wherever there are shallows and flats. Their average weight runs between 3 and 5 pounds. A 5- to 9-pound bonefish is considered large, and above 9 a whopper. The world's record is 19¼ pounds, measuring 3 feet 3⅝ inches long with a girth of 17 inches. It was caught in an area where bonefish is not yet sport fishing—Zululand, South Africa—on May 26, 1962.

The table below gives weights for 18- to 37-inch fish. These weights are of course approximate, as the fish often vary in girth.

Length (inches)	Weight (pounds)	Length (inches)	Weight (pounds)
18	3.5	28	8.6
19	3.8	29	9.6
20	4.1	30	10.8
21	4.6	31	11.9
22	5.1	32	13.0
23	5.5	33	14.4
24	6.0	34	15.6
25	6.5	35	16.8
26	7.2	36	18.0
27	7.7	37	19.2

The previous world's record fish weighed 18 pounds 2 ounces and was caught in Hawaii; before that Bermuda held the honor. Fifteen-pound fish are caught each year in the Bahamas and in the Florida Keys. Thus it is apparent that the habitat of *Albula vulpes* is worldwide.

Bonefish feed on flats and in shallows, usually on the last of the ebb and the beginning of the flood tides. Their food consists of clams, crabs, sand

The bonefish has a hard, bony snout for digging in the sand.

This is the tongue of a bonefish, covered with pearl-like beads that aid in crushing clams and crabs.

worms, shrimp, small mollusks, and fish, as well as sand to aid in digestion. The tongue and roof of the mouth are covered with countless small round beads which look like pearls. This formation is capable of flattening the toughest clam, and back of the tongue on both sides there are powerful crushers to complete the job of disintegration. Obviously, no hook will penetrate the armor completely, but if a bonefish is hooked in the seedlike construction, the hook will often hold long enough to land the fish, and fortunately the bonefish usually swims with its mouth closed. (I have caught many in this manner only to have the hook fall out when the fish is netted and the line has slackened.) In playing such a hooked fish the bonefisherman's only tactic is to keep as much tension as possible, since any slack will almost always mean a lost fish. Thus it is always best to strike a bonefish when its head is turned or it is sideways to you; then the hook will penetrate the tough, fleshy part of the mouth.

Bonefish feed on the bottom in grass and also in mud or sand. When their heads are down feeding, and the water is sufficiently shallow, their tails wave in the air. This is called "tailing." Mud stirred up by feeding fish is referred to as "mudding." These tell-

This grassy bottom is a typical feeding area for bonefish.

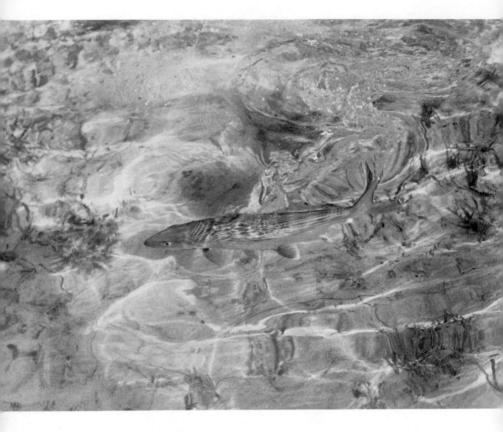

This bonefish feeding in shallow water typically has its head down and tail waving in air.

tale characteristics enable a guide with trained vision to locate the fish sometimes as far off as 100 yards if the visibility is good; that is, bright sun, preferably at your back, and reasonably calm water. Blind casting in deep water is not much fun and is seldom productive unless bonefish are plentiful. When there is a large area of muddy water indicating a sizable school of feeding fish, however, a cast into the water will sometimes produce a fish.

Occasionally when working a flat you will come across a traveling sting ray, stirring up mud and sand as its flippers fan the bottom. It's a good idea to cast into the mud, for bonefish often trail rays, picking up food in the wake.

The waving tails make it possible to spot a feeding school a long way off.

Bait,
Wiggle Jig,
and Fly

I am often asked, "What is the best way to catch bonefish?" If you really want to know the best way to catch the *most* bonefish that's a different matter. To catch the *most* bonefish I'd say use bait, and list baits in the order of their effectiveness: crawfish or crab, shrimp, soldier crab, and, finally, conch. By and large bait fishing will result in the most fish numerically, but not the best fishing spiritually. As to the methods and tactics of catching bonefish by bait, I recommend letting the fish do most of the work, especially if chum or "baiting up" is used. The bonefish will find the bait with its keen nose, and then if it's in the mood, it'll grab it and run. The angler snubs but not too hard, and usually that's all there is to it. The method of playing a hooked fish is pretty much the same whether it is caught on bait, jig, spinner, or fly.

A second effective method of catching bonefish is with a spinning rod and a spinning lure such as a wiggle jig or weighted fly. In this instance it isn't so much the lure or its color that counts as the way it is manipulated in the water. The best technique is to jump or jig it in short hops, say a foot or two at a time with pauses in between. These pauses will permit the lure to sink to the bottom, and the jig will jump up and forward in the manner of a shrimp trying to escape. This action is calculated to arouse the interest of the bonefish. When the fish shows this interest and follows the lure it is quite important to give it quicker action, which frequently excites the fish to the point of attack.

In spinning for bonefish the accuracy of the cast is very important. Some people prefer an overhead cast, but in my opinion a side cast is more effective. An overhead cast, being higher in the air, allows the wind to blow the lure off course so that it lands off target, and, the higher the cast above the water, the more conspicuous it is to the fish. The target for a spinning lure should be from 7 to 10 feet in front of the bonefish's eyes. Anything closer than 7 feet would almost always frighten the fish. Also, a cast behind the fish or over 5 feet off on either side would probably not be seen.

Another advantage to the side cast is that the lure hits the water with less splash or commotion than with an overhead cast, and this is important. There is one other factor which also plays a great part in

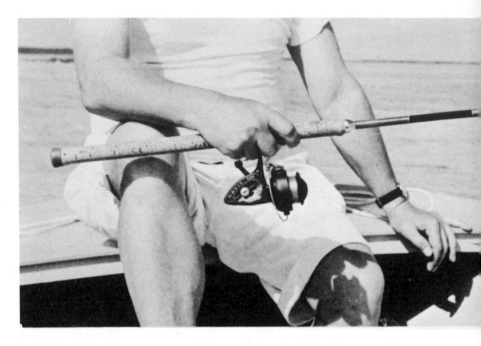

One secret of accurate casting with spinning tackle is maintaining a proper grip on the line between the first and second joints of the index finger.

spinning accuracy, namely, the initial control of the line with the index finger. The line should be held midway between the first joint and the end of the finger. If it is at the crease between the first and second joints it will frequently catch in the crease, assuring a bungled cast. The release of the line at the proper instant is an all-important factor in attaining accuracy. If the line is held too long the lure will end up with a splash right in front of the angler, and if it is released prematurely the lure will sail off into the air at right angles.

The most sporting method of catching bonefish is fly fishing. This requires more fishing skill than the other methods, and is the most rewarding. The problem is to get the fly before the fish with the minimum of commotion and the maximum of speed. The movement of the fly should be similar to the motion of jigs: a series of short hops in the water. A no. 4 fly will take 7 seconds to sink 12 inches. As it nears the bottom it becomes more tempting, and as the fish takes interest in the fly, its movement should be accelerated.

Bonefish
Psychology

Bonefish are extremely nervous, and the slightest sound or movement in the water or overhead will flush them. This is called "spooking." A flock of snipe flying over a flat will stampede a nearby school of fish. They scatter in all directions, only to rejoin the school later. This characteristic of bonefish is unusual among fishes, and it makes their pursuit more difficult as well as more exciting. When hooked a bonefish will run like lightning for deep water or for mangroves or coral formations within 100 or so yards. To hold firm on this initial run is almost always fatal. An 8-pound test line will be snapped like a violin string even by a 3-pound fish. That such a small fish can develop a breaking power two or three times its own weight is extraordinary.

Joe Brooks, who rates the bonefish among the greatest of game fish, describes it in the same letter I have already quoted as a valiant fighter which almost breaks its heart in that first wild rush for escape.

Any bonefish is great, but they are at their best in shallow water where their headlong flight across the flats is something to marvel at. In deep water they are just another fish, and most anglers do not go for them in deep water, seeking them out instead on their feeding grounds on the shallow flats. In such a case, in water from six to twelve inches deep, the bonefish is one of the most difficult fish in the world to take on a fly. There have been a few places I've fished where this had not proven true—new, unfished waters, where I've seen a bonefish take a fly 15 feet from the skiff, seemingly not frightened of us at all. But the next time we came back it was a different story. They were difficult to take.

Feeding close to the bottom of a flat that is either sandy or muddy, bonefish are aided in getting away by mangrove shoots, shells, bits of coral, sponges, etc. A monofilament line, or gut leader, under tension coming in contact with any of these will part like a thread. By holding his rod as high as possible, to keep the fish's chin off the bottom, the angler can minimize this danger. At the same time the boatman poles toward the fish to shorten the line as much as possible, further reducing opportunities for contact with cutting edges.

Mangroves at low tide, an ideal spot for a hooked bonefish to break a line.

Bonefish rarely jump, except in unusual circumstances such as when a hooked bonefish is attacked by a barracuda. In such a predicament the angler should immediately release all tension on the line to enable the bonefish to escape through its speed and dodging ability. If tension is maintained it is too handicapped to avoid the attack.

It is incredible how quickly a shark or barracuda will appear when a bonefish is hooked. The same thing happens in fishing for wahoo—shark apparently sense when a fish is in trouble and vulnerable to attack. An article by Warren Wisby in *Sea Frontiers*, February 1964, published by the International Oceanographic Foundation, reported on a number of laboratory tests which were conducted to determine the reasons for the phenomenon. The findings indicated that when any fish, either by change of color or action, departed from its normal behavior, it became conspicuous not only to predators but to others of its own species. One of the experiments was made on a small catfish (*Synodontis* sp.) which normally swims upside down.

When in this position its belly is darker than its back. This coloration is the reverse of that found in fishes which swim right side up but the effect is the same; the surface which is on top is dark and the bottom surface is light. If food is now placed on the bottom of the aquarium, it becomes necessary for the catfish to turn over in order to eat. When this happens it attracts the attention of every other aquarium inmate. Larger fish nip at it and smaller ones stare. As evidence of its discomfort it soon reverses its coloration and retains it until it again assumes the normal upside-down position.

Symptoms of distress then become a mechanism for imparting information and can, therefore, be considered communication. It is obvious that fishes may signal their distress by visual means. What other symptoms of trouble might a predator detect? Violent struggling may cause vibrations which are meaningful to a hungry predator. These signals are probably detectable at a much greater distance than that over which vision alone would be effective. Also, if an injury occurs which releases blood the incident could be detected by any predator with a good nose.

While bonefish do not jump, they do everything else to frustrate their opponent. They are perpetual motion, fighting every second with long runs or circling the boat or sometimes heading straight for the angler to gain some slack. Because of this exhausting play the fight is often over within five to fifteen minutes, when the fish is netted without a struggle. I have often seen them so exhausted that they will die without a flop when laid in the boat.

If released after netting they will lie on their sides, and often if left that way they will die. The remedy for this is simple and effective: artificial respiration. If a bonefish is taken by the tail and slowly thrust forward and backward the action of the water will open and close the gills, thereby forcing the passage of water (breathing to a fish). After a couple of minutes the fish will assume an upright, normal position, and the tail will start to wag.

Giving an exhausted bonefish artificial respiration before releasing it.

Sporting History
of Bonefish

Whereas most gamefish are members of large families, the bonefish is the only species of the family Albulidae. Fishing for them with rod and reel was first discovered in 1891, but it was not until thirty-five years later that its popularity as a sport fish began to be appreciated.

The first recorded bonefish to be landed with rod and reel was caught by J. B. McFerran of Louisville, Kentucky, in 1891. W. H. Gregg describes the adventure in *Where, When and How to Catch Fish on the East Coast of Florida* (Buffalo and New York: The Matthews-Northrup Works, 1902).

McFerran had been fishing in Florida for some time before he knew there was such a creature as the bonefish. He learned of its existence in casual conversation with a Coconut Grove storekeeper who asked him if he had ever caught a bonefish. When he admitted that he was not familiar with it, the proprietor stepped to the door and pointing across Biscayne Bay to Coco Plum Point said: "There at the flooding of the tide, close up to the shore where the water will scarcely cover their backs, you will find them."

Intrigued, the Louisville sportsman rowed out to the point where, after two hours of fishing in eight or nine inches of water, he began to feel as if he had been made the butt of a joke. He started to reel in his line when he detected five or six shadows moving rapidly across the flat and he knew that he was confronted with "a distinctly new proposition in the piscatorial line." But his time was up and he had to leave without sampling the fighting qualities of the "white fox."

The following February he was back at Coconut Grove prepared to come to grips with the elusive will-o'-the-wisp of the banks come hell or high water.

After making several inquiries he could learn of no one who had ever caught "Little Alby" with rod and reel. The local people told him it could not be done. The only way that bonefish could be taken they claimed with with grains (a two- or three-pronged spear) and occasionally with a handline, the hook baited with conch, and the thrower stooping down to make the toss.

Nothing daunted, he fished the floodtide for three weeks with nary a pickup. He could see the fish by the hundreds, but no sooner did he get within casting range of a school than the splash made by the lead sinker would send every mother's son off like the wind. Discouraged—he was about to call it off when he discovered about an acre of bare sand bottom flanked by a small channel, beyond which was a shallow bay covered with a heavy growth of grass.

"Put me on the far side of that bare spot," he told his boatman, "and if we cannot catch one coming out of that channel we will give it up and put out for Key West."

About ten minutes after the boat had been moved and McFerran had made a cast, leaving the bait lie a little way from the channel, eight or ten bonefish eased onto the bank and in five minutes the angler had his fish! He had been fishing in many waters, near and far, salt and fresh, but here, according to him, "was a sensation indeed, a new edition of chain lightning, and that greased."

McFerran closed his letter to Gregg with these words: "I verily believe that, pound for pound, the Bonefish is, far and away, the King of all swimmers and the only objection I can urge against him is that an experience with him forever disqualifies one for all other fishing." To which hundreds of anglers say, "Amen!"

It was not until 1924 that there is any record of a bonefish being caught on a fly rod. This took place on one of the Florida Keys, and it was caught by accident by a snapper fisherman. At any rate, I think it can truthfully be stated that the bonefish became a sport fish on the Florida Keys, as far as flyfishermen are concerned. Joe Brooks, Ted Williams, Lee Wulff, and many other anglers all took their degrees as B.A.s (bonefish addicts) on the Florida Keys.

It was in the early 1930's that I caught my first bonefish. I was in Florida and was talking to the great angler George La Branch, a fellow member of the Anglers Club of New York, and he asked me if I knew what a bonefish was. I admitted I had never even heard of bonefish. He then suggested that I give bonefishing a try and referred me to a guide named Bill Smith.

The next day Bill took us to a slick at the edge of a sand bank and proceeded to bait the place up with some chopped-up conch. My rod was a short bait-casting rod with a free-running, take-apart reel.

The author and his favorite guide, Bonefish Joe, with a
10-pound bonefish—the fly-rod record for the Bahamas.

It wasn't long before I had a bite, nothing spectacular, but I struck. I had no drag on the reel to keep it from back lashing, so I attempted to slow down the speed of the braided line with my thumb on the reel. It was as if a red-hot coal had hit my thumb. It only took a few seconds to remove the skin from my thumb, and the ensuing backlash immediately broke the line like a piece of thread.

The next day George La Branch lent me a leather thumb stall. This did the trick, and my first bonefish was finally hauled in.

Bill Smith, incidentally, had a daughter named Bonnie who took to bonefishing with a fly rod as a duck takes to water, and she became a famous fishing guide, specializing in flycasting. Of late years she has been devoting her entire time, I believe, to teaching the art of flyfishing, especially for bonefish.

Still-Fishing, Skiff Fishing, and Wading

Before discussing how to fish for bonefish let us first decide what kind of fishing we want.

At the bottom of the sport scale comes still-fishing, which calls for a boat with an anchor. (Two anchors are better, as they will keep the boat from swinging.) The first step is to scatter bits of conch or crawfish around the immediate area. This should be done at low tide before the turn. For this kind of fishing one needs only a bait-casting rod, with a free-running reel and a drag. The reel should hold at least 200 yards of 6 to 9 threadline. While a small sinker is generally used to facilitate casting out the bait, no sinker at all is preferable. A spinning rod can also be used for still-fishing, and the reel should hold at least 200 yards of 10-pound-test monofilament line.

Skiff fishing. Here Mrs. Babson casts to a pair of tailing bonefish that the skiff has silently tracked.

Now place your bait—a piece of crawfish, soldier crab, shrimp, or conch—in the path of the incoming tide where bonefish enter the flat through a shallow channel. This method of fishing for bonefish prevails throughout the world with natives, who usually spurn a rod in favor of a handline.

An alternative to still-fishing, and much more sport, is to have a skilled boatman or guide pole a skiff over the shallows. This must be done soundlessly. When a fish is observed the angler casts his bait some 10 to 15 feet in front of the oncoming fish. Skiff fishing is generally the most rewarding as it is easier and quieter to be poled over the flat than to maneuver yourself through the water to get within casting distance of feeding bonefish. Thus, you can present your lure to more fish. In addition, the added height provided by the boat enables you to see fish at a greater distance, and the rod is held higher, thereby minimizing the hazards of bottom growths. Finally, if a whopper is hooked it is easier to follow by boat than on foot, especially if the fish heads for deep water.

Nevertheless, the most exciting method is to wade the flats. This is possible when the bottom is hard and footing reasonably good; it should not be attempted when the bottom is soft or marly, as there are dangers of extra soft spots or even quicksand. In wading you must go very slowly and when approaching the fish step high over the water to diminish noise.

Wading the flats is even more exciting than skiff fishing, and it requires great skill. Here Mrs. Babson locates her quarry and casts.

The guide stands ready with the net as Mrs. Babson brings a tired bonefish in.

Wading along on a colorful flat after bonefish is just as much fun and maybe more than fishing from a skiff, but to be fair, I must mention the drawbacks to wading. First, the range of visibility is nothing like as good in wading as it is from a boat, for the simple reason that when an angler is standing up in the bottom of a boat his eyes are about 2 feet higher above water level than when he is wading up to his knees in water. This makes a big difference in the clarity of your vision. If you stand up on the seat of the boat, which is where the guide stands, you have still another extra foot of height. The second disadvantage to wading is that it is noisy. The sound of the water splashing and swirling around your legs can be heard by a bonefish a long way off, very much farther than sound above water. A third handicap to wading, unless you use a spinning rod, is the difficulty of controlling the extra coil of casting line which you need available for speed in getting out your cast. It's hard enough to keep 20 feet of line in the bottom of a boat out of the way of your feet and other things that catch, but if it's loose in the water, it gets around your legs and tangles itself with bottom growth. Lastly, when a fish is hooked, you can hold your line up 2 or 3 extra feet in the air. That helps tremendously to keep the line off the bottom and away from various shells and growths which can cut your leader.

Spinning Tackle

A recent development in bonefishing is to dispense with bait entirely. Using a spinning rod and weighted flies or spinning lure, the angler wades the flats or searches for the elusive fish from the slowly poled skiff. The most popular rod for spinning-rod fishing is a 6½- or 7-foot split-bamboo or glass spinning rod with medium-stiff action. I prefer the 7-foot rod as it gives me better accuracy and distance, also I can "shoot" the line into the wind more effectively than with shorter or lighter rods. The rod weight should be about 4 ounces. I like to have two rods in the boat, with lures of different design or color. The extra rod is a safety measure, since a loop, knot, or bird's nest tangle may develop in the line in use. Like the second barrel of a shotgun, it is mighty comforting to have another rod ready for instant action. I know of no more frustrating experience than to be in casting distance of a school of bonefish and have a loop, knot, or tangle in the line. One must never cast under these conditions because it is virtually im-

A bonefish caught by the wading method on spinning tackle.

possible to present a lure properly with a tangled line, and if the fish should by chance get hooked, a knot in nylon line is almost sure to break at the wrong moment.

There are many spinning reels available, and new innovations are constantly on the market. At present there are a number of reels in which the line releases from a cone that is advertised as anti-backlash. I question the validity of the claim that such reels are proof against backlash. Then there are baleless reels with automatic pickups and with various methods of releasing the line for casting. While some of these innovations may be very efficient, I generally like a reel that does not conceal the line—I like to see it on the spool and be able to detect loops and knots before they cause trouble. Also, I like reels that do not require constant cleaning and lubrication to keep from freezing when used in salt water. No matter how careful one is, it is almost impossible to protect reels from salt spray. And it is a nuisance to wash reels in fresh water each time they are used. The Orvis Model 100 is my favorite for bonefish spinning. I have five, and they have had plenty of wear. After a season, if cleaned and oiled and put away in a dry place they are as good as new the next year. Some of these reels have been used winter after winter for a dozen years and are still going strong.

Lures are legion. While impossible to cite them all, a few general hints are in order. They should not weigh over one-ninth of an ounce. (A few heavier might be kept on hand for use against heavy wind. I have used a Dunmore fly with the body weighted to one-ninth ounce.) Then there are wiggle jigs, which are bucktail or streamer flies with a flat

A bonefish hooked on a wiggle jig. A hook in the side of the mouth will seldom pull out.

colored head. They come in two weights, one-ninth ounce and one-fourth ounce. I prefer the lighter. Some flies with a spinner attached are now being made, and they are quite effective in very shallow water—they do not seem to get snagged in the grass as often as wiggle jigs. The prime consideration is to use flies that are right for the depth of the water.

Joe Brooks uses white bucktails during the winter months and streamers the rest of the year. He believes in carrying a minimum of patterns which have proved themselves. He concentrates on Upperman streamer flies nos. 101, 102, 103, 104, and 107; for bucktails, Upperman nos. 105 and 106.

Most lures and flies are made in several colors and combinations of colors. The prevailing ones are white, yellow, pink, brown, and black, although I believe that the color is not as important as the presentation. Generally, I prefer a dark fly on a light bottom and a light fly on a dark or grassy bottom. White, yellow, and pink do especially well, though the pink should not be too red. I suspect a bonefish mistakes it for a shrimp. Incidentally, Brooks has developed a small pink fly for fly rods that is supposed to resemble a shrimp.

Spinning Lures

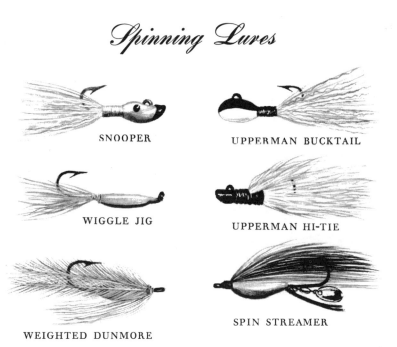

SNOOPER

UPPERMAN BUCKTAIL

WIGGLE JIG

UPPERMAN HI-TIE

WEIGHTED DUNMORE

SPIN STREAMER

Flyfishing Tackle

The most exciting, the most difficult, but the sportiest and most rewarding way of all to fish for bonefish is by fly rod. When the wind is no more than 8 miles per hour I always use a fly rod. (The use of a fly in very windy weather is too frustrating.) When bonefish are tailing and are downwind, or when the water is fairly calm and the visibility good and not murky, is the best time to use the fly rod. If it is skillfully handled I believe it is as productive, and often more so, than spinning with metal lures. Because of its weight the spinning lure is bound to splash when it hits the water, and bonefish can hear the disturbance at a surprising distance. Because the weight of an artificial fly is negligible, when presented properly it

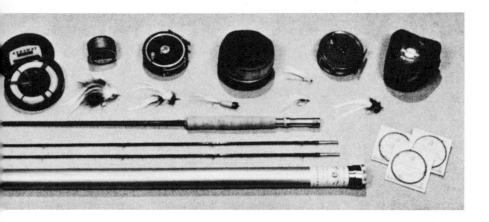

Tackle for flyfishing.

will make no splash at all, and it can be dropped
closer to the fish or, indeed, right at them. While I
love to hear the reel scream when the bonefish takes
its run, alas, it is too noisy, and a silent and adjustable drag is preferable.

The best fly rod for bonefishing is a 9-foot 6-ounce
rod with slow action for power casts. I prefer an
Orvis Battenkill, which I also find ideal for salmon
fishing. The Orvis Battenkill is not too heavy, especially when used with a well-greased line or one of
the new hollow, floating lines, such as the Gladdings
"Aerofloat." It is an expensive rod to purchase and
maintain, however. After one winter in the tropics,
in spite of good care, it usually needs a complete re-
finishing. Consequently I had a rodmaker attempt to
duplicate its action in glass. The result was sur-
prisingly good.

A good salmon reel with a torpedo headline, 200
yards of backing, and a 9-foot tapered leader and you

Fly Rod Lures

PINK SHRIMP

DUNMORE

MILLS

WOOLEY WORM

YELLOW MARABOU

GREY GHOST

are set for an exciting experience with bonefish—
if all conditions are right and the fish are there and
in a biting mood.

When a bonefish is hooked on a fly rod the technique for playing it is similar to that with a spinning
outfit. There is only one difference: With the stronger
leader greater strain can be brought to bear on the
fish and consequently you have a better chance of
keeping it out of any nearby mangroves. And if the

bonefish *does* run afoul, the heavier line of different material will not cut so readily as monofilament nylon, even though chances are you will still be the loser.

Hook size is very important in fly fishing for bonefish. A light hook is essential when fishing in the shallow waters of the flats, as a heavy hook sinks too quickly and often gets snagged on the bottom. I usually use a no. 4 size. Rusty hooks should be avoided at all costs, for they will discolor the feathers and bucktails of your jigs and flies, and a rusty hook is apt to break in the bonefish's crushers.

Line

Clinch Knot

There are a number of suitable knots for fastening lines or flies to monofilament lines, for joining monofilament lines together, or for mending breaks. But two are outstanding: the clinch knot and the blood or barrel knot.

Blood Knot

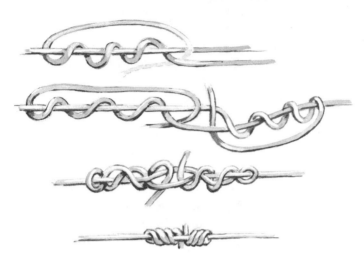

To tie a clinch knot, place the end of the leader through the eye of the lure or fly, double it back against itself, and wind it around the line or leader five times. Then thrust the end between the eye of the lure and the first coil. For added safety insert the end back through the loop, and pull it tight.

The blood or barrel knot is best for joining gut or nylon. It is something like the clinch knot. Each line is wound around the other and the ends are tucked through and pulled tight. Both knots are shown in the accompanying diagram.

The barrel knot is shown with only three turns for each line, but James Barhydt, head of the fishing-line department at Du Pont, told me that in tying barrel knots five turns are best; he added that four would sacrifice 20 percent of the strength, and that six turns would not produce any added breaking strength. (A knot cannot add strength to any line, and, of course, is the weakest spot on an undamaged line.) Mr. Barhydt felt that any knot affects the line strength adversely by approximately 8 percent; for example, an 8-pound-test line with a knot has a fishing strength of about 7½ pounds.

Nylon has a tendency to slip sometimes, but it rarely happens with a clinch knot. If you want to be doubly safe, tie an ordinary granny knot at the end and pull it tight; it will never pull through. Some anglers burn the tip end of the leader with a cigarette butt instead of tying the granny knot, putting a bead on the line that won't slip.

When it comes to spinning lines I prefer an 8-pound-test monofilament. There are many excellent makes on the market. I happen to use Stren, made by Du Pont. Up to the present writing I believe it has the smallest diameter, the least stretch, and the greatest uniformity of tensile strength of all.

Many bonefishermen prefer 6-pound-test line, and there is no doubt that 6-pound-test line will permit 20 or 30 percent extra casting distance. But when the big fellow, 7 or 8 pounds, runs and heads toward the distant mangroves or starts toward treacherous underwater coral, the extra 2 pounds of tensile strength are mighty comforting to have on the reel.

I have discovered that an undamaged line improves with use. It becomes more pliable and less springy or kinky. As a precaution, however, I have found it worthwhile after a few hours fishing, especially if a fish or two have been caught, to cut a foot or so off the line and retie the lure. It is also a good plan to trail 100 yards of line, without lure attached, behind the boat on the way home. This will eliminate kinky tendencies which are almost sure to develop, especially if several fish have been caught.

As important as any other equipment are polaroid glasses to cut glare. The author also wears a surgeon's mask as protection against sunburn.

Recently, Du Pont laboratories announced a new fluorescent monofilament spinning line which combines outstanding visibility to the fisherman and low visibility to the fish. The angler is able to see the line clearly as it arches out over the water, giving him better control of the line. Fish, on the other hand, cannot distinguish the blue fluorescent line, which blends with the bright undersurface of the water.

Speaking of visibility, sunglasses are so essential to the bonefisherman that it is important to include them as necessary equipment. Even with a good pair of eyes, it is hard to see bonefish as they steal over the white shallows; but when there are ripples on the water, which is usually the case, the light reflections and the myriads of shadows caused by aquatic growths make bonefish detection much more difficult. Polaroid glasses cut through the reflections and greatly aid vision.

Guides Good and Bad

Most books on fishing say nothing about guides. Some kinds of fishing do not require guides, such as surf casting or wading a trout stream. But in most fishing, where a boat, canoe, or skiff is needed, a guide is quite necessary. The guide's degree of usefulness depends first of all on his skill in handling the boat, though his knowledge of the water and his personality are important too.

I have never tried to count the guides I have had in various parts of the world during the past several years, but there may have been close to a hundred. Some were good and some weren't. I know guides so understanding and helpful and such good company that even a fishless day with them could be a delightful experience. On the other hand, I have had guides who were so disagreeable and ornery that it was a formidable ordeal to stay in the boat with them, regardless of how good the fishing was. I recall a surly Indian in the interior of Quebec, miles from habitation. He spoke no English, just a mixture of French and Indian. He answered my every attempt at conversation with the word *malade* which means "sick," and I never did discover if he meant me or himself. Among my experiences with guides I put him at the very bottom of the totem pole.

Then there are guides who like to take along a little flask on the side, which they artfully explain is for good luck. This usually means their luck and not mine. If the fish are not biting, they take a furtive swig "for luck," and when we catch an extra-large fish they celebate.

However, I would say that the general average of guides is good, and occasionally one finds a man who has all the qualifications and is a real pro. A bonefish guide must be able to maneuver his bonefish boat with speed and without a sound. His reactions must be with lightning speed. Such a guide is Bonefish Joe. Once when I was fishing with him I was playing a good-size bonefish which had made its first run and was on the way to a second trip, when the line suddenly parted. "He's off!" I said. Joe made one leap like a giant frog and landed in the water just in front of the boat. There was the white floating line slowly moving away. He picked it up and called to me to pick up the backing line in the water right alongside of the boat. "Quick, quick, quick!" he shouted. I handed him the backing line, which had come unspliced from the casting line. Between his two hands and his mouth he managed to tie the two lines together in a flash just as the fish started on its next run. When the line had parted and the tension stopped, the fish had apparently

Bonefish Joe, in front of the author's Bahamas cottage with a 9³/₄-pounder.

taken advantage of the pause for a breather, just long enough for Joe to tie the lines together. The ending was a happy one as Joe finally lifted him into the boat. (Moral: Occasionally test where the backing is spliced to the casting line, as it can pull apart in time, no matter how well spliced.)

Another qualification has to do with the eyes. A guide has to see everything almost at once. I spend a lot of time looking for bonefish as they feed or swim slowly along a sandy flat or grassy bottom, but it is very rare that I can see a fish before Joe. Just why Joe and other native Bahamans can see so much better than white men, I can't understand. I asked Joe, and he explained that it was because he was accustomed to look for things through the water. He added that white men look at the surface instead of looking at the bottom through the water.

When passing through deeper water on the way to a flat, Joe is full of conversation, and sometime he bursts into song. My son made up some verses for one of Joe's tunes:

BONEFISH JOE'S TRACKING SONG
Bonefish, bonefish, where you at?
No use to hide from me.
You must be on this sandy flat
Or perhaps behind that cay.

I see the sign where you been here
The mud where you been digging.
Bonefish, you better have a care
Cause I'm comin' wiggle jigging.

Bonefish, bonefish, don't you spook,
You're hungry as a pig.
Bye and bye the clouds will pass the sun,
Then you will meet my jig.

"He's at 11:30 now, about 50 feet, going to the left..."

But on the flat, Joe stands right behind me and keeps whispering in my ear. His first task is to show me the fish, and he does this by giving his directions in terms of the hands of a clock. The bow is 12 o'clock. With one hand pointed at the fish, Joe might say, "He's at 11:30 now, about 50 feet going to the left, get your false casts out to the side. Now cast about 10 o'clock, once again same place, now again a little more to the left . . . good." Then anything can happen.

As the day goes on and the sun starts to sink, I look at my watch. Joe seems to sense what I'm doing. "Don't look at dat watch, wait till we catch two more fish." Joe is never ready to go home. If our luck has been poor, he says, "Let's try again—we can't go home without any. Just another fifteen minutes." If, on the other hand, we have done well, he will say, "We can't stop now, the fishing's too good. Just one more try."

Of course, Joe is not the only good guide with whom I have fished for bonefish. I know there are many excellent guides elsewhere too. Bonefish Sam, for instance, has a fine reputation at Bimini. I have heard lots about him but have never met him. Ted Williams has a guide at Islamorada in Florida and his name is Jimmy Albright. Ted is as good at bone-fishing as he is on a baseball diamond, and any guide who has fished with him as long as Albright certainly must know all the tricks of catching bones and a lot more that they don't divulge. But Bonefish Joe is my favorite, and that is why his name occurs so frequently when I discuss guides and tactics.

With all Joe's merits, no one is perfect. There is one habit he has which is something to try one's soul. I have gotten used to it now, so it doesn't bother me any more. Suppose I have just hooked a nice bonefish—I haven't seen it as yet, but Joe has and says it will go 7 pounds. The fish makes its first run and there is nothing to do but let it go. On the second run, it circles and heads for the deep water. Suddenly the line slacks. "He's gone, Joe," I say, and sure enough I reel in and find the leader broken in what looks like the remains of a knot. (Moral: Always inspect leaders for knots and never cast one with a knot in it.) "Too bad," says Joe, and a long and painful silence follows. After a while he says, more or less to himself, "Eight pounds, I believe." I say nothing but do a lot of restrained thinking. We take up our fishing and proceed. Complete silence for another few minutes. Then Joe murmurs again, mostly to himself but loud enough to hear, "Could have gone 8½ pounds." Eventually we have better luck and the lost fish seems to be forgotten. But on landing at the dock there are always a few friends gathered to see what luck we have had—and Joe announces in a loud voice, "Mr. Babson just lost a 9½ pounder."

But I cannot overemphasize the value of a guide like Joe. For twenty-five years I experimented with all the various ways to catch bonefish: still-fishing with bait, spinning with various types of hardware, weighted flies, wiggle jigs, wading, drifting, stalking with fly rod, etc. I flattered myself into believing that I had become something of an expert. But that was before I met Bonefish Joe, guide extraordinary. It was he who enabled me to refine the techniques I had started.

An expert guide is more necessary to the bonefisherman than to other kinds of anglers. A bonefish guide must be able to push a light skiff silently against a strong wind over shallow flats, and he must be endowed with unusually keen eyesight. He must be able to interpret the telltale signs that a feeding bonefish leaves on the bottom, then accurately second-guess its subsequent movements. Finally, of course, he needs an agreeable personality.

Indeed, the relationship between sportsman and boatman or guide must be that of a team working

together in a common aim. In this connection I would say that 70 percent of successful bonefishing depends on the guide, 15 percent on the angler and his equipment, and 15 percent on luck.

Another exceptional guide of my acquaintance is Glen Tatum. A master of understatement, he is the direct opposite of Joe. Glen seldom speaks, but when he does, mark well what he says. Even when he actually sees a lurking bonefish he will say quietly and with restraint, "Mr. Babson, I think there's two bonefish at 2:30 o'clock about 40 feet and going to the left." That's all he says. The trick now is to deliver the cast without delay about 10 feet in front of the fish.

Glen Tatum, bonefish guide and captain of the yacht Hope.

I have seen, talked, and fished with many experienced and fine anglers, and not one of them, including myself, could match the vision of Joe and other Bahamans in seeing through the water. Without polaroid glasses one cannot read the signs on the bottom or analyze the color changes in the water. I have seen Joe take out many neophytes, who have never caught a fish of any kind, and they will come in with one or more bonefish. An experienced fisherman on his own or with an inexperienced boatman will come in empty-handed.

Guides in Action

Let's go out with Joe for a typical morning's fishing under reasonably favorable conditions: good sun (not too many clouds), a favorable wind not exceeding 10 or 12 miles an hour, and air temperature not under 70°F. It is half tide, say 2 or 3 feet on the flats. Joe is at my side in the bow, looking, forever looking, at the bottom. He poles the boat very slowly and in absolute silence. If possible, he will get upwind and drift sideways (this is far better than drifting head on, as there is no wave slap on the sides of the boat). His pole never touches the side—that could scare away any nearby bonefish, as they are hypersensitive to sounds transmitted through the water.

Joe whispers as he goes along, partly to his passenger, partly to himself. "There's been a few bones here, maybe six or so—not many."

*Bonefish Joe scouts for fish. Almost always he sees them
before his passengers.*

"How do you know that, Joe?"

"By the number of holes in the sand where they
stick their noses in for food. If it was a school of a
dozen or more, the holes would be much closer together, maybe a foot apart. They gone 'bout an hour
by now."

"How do you figure that?"

"On account of the color of the mussed-up sand.
When it's fresh it's real bluish, but by the time the
tide change the blue is all gone. I tell the time by

the shade of color. Also, I tell by the sharpness of the edges of the hole: The fresher the sign the sharper the edges. After an hour or so the movement of the water smooths out the edges. These fish have gone that way to the mangroves."

"You mean you can tell which way they went?"

"Yes, the bonefish snout is sharp on the top and wide underneath—all those holes show the narrow part pointing toward the mangroves. Let's go to Cole Point Flat. I think they is more bonefish there."

So we go on to Cole Point Flat, stopping our outboard at least 200 yards away. Again Joe scans the bottom as we creep over the flats. I can see nothing. After a while Joe whispers tensely, "A big school been here 'bout fifteen minutes ago. They not far off?"

"What makes you think that, Joe?"

"The water is a little smoky. See!"

"Oh, yes," I lie, but I can see no difference. Ever so slowly, we move on as Joe becomes even more excited. "Don't you see that fresh mudlike yellow smoke?" he says. And sure enough, now that it is pointed out, I can detect a faintly murky appearance. Joe now points about 50 feet ahead where a distinct milky area dulls the usual crystal clearness of the water.

"Now," says Joe, "we got to get a double." To my son Stanley, who is with us, he says, "Get ready and take the first cast, right over there on the right, 2 o'clock, about 40 feet." And to me, "Get ready, don't cast till I say so. They'll probably turn left and cross our bow." He says to Stan, "Now, cast— good! Now jig, leave it now, jig, jig again, reel a bit, now jig, you got him." Then to me, "Over there

Joe points the way to the bonefish, and the angler makes his cast.

The fish is hooked. The rod is held low so that if the hook gives the lure will not jump out of the water, for the fish may strike again if the lure is still visible.

Now the fish makes its first long run, and the rod is held high to keep the line off the bottom.

Brought to the net, the fish is still capable of a last flurry, so the net must be handled very carefully.

The net is quickly raised, and one battle is over— though the fish, wiser but unharmed, may be released to fight again.

50 feet, 11 o'clock, jig, jig—reel in fast, reel and cast again, nine o'clock, now jig, rest, jig—you got him!"

To illustrate determination an experience comes to mind of a bonefisherman who had hooked a fairly large bonefish which had headed for a clump of mangroves some 150 yards distant. Before reaching the mangroves, however, the fish appeared to slow down. Anxious to regain some line, the angler tightened the drag slightly and started to reel in. He reeled and reeled but did not seem to recover any line. Suddenly he realized that the line on the reel had disappeared. Either it was not fastened to the core of the reel or the terminal knot had slipped out, as is common with an improperly tied monofilament line. At any rate there was the limp rod, the empty reel, and the departed fish.

Again Bonefish Joe was the guide, and when he saw what had happened he shouted, "I'll get him!" He jumped into the knee-deep water, headed for the mangroves 100 yards away, and disappeared from sight. Five minutes passed, then ten, before a shout came from the heart of the mangroves. "We got him—'bout 5 pounds." A few minutes later Joe reached the skiff and laid a 5 pounder on the bottom with 200 yards of line trailing behind.

Joe knew the direction the fish had taken when it headed for the mangroves. Once there he waded across the fish's path, shuffling his feet along the muddy bottom. When he felt the line on his ankles he reached down and picked it up. The fish had stopped its initial run, and feeling no pull of line had paused for a breather. By tracking the line in and out over and under and around the mangroves he came to a water level of only a few inches deep,

Bonefish Joe goes into the mangroves after a fish that has emptied a reel and gone off with the line.

and there the bonefish was trying desperately to free itself in the shallow water. But the fish did not have a chance when Joe pounced on it.

I think I can suggest one answer to the question of why bonefishing takes such a hold on reasonably normal anglers. I think it results from the special challenge of fishing with an all-seeing and all-knowing guide. The fisherman wants to excel in his own right, instead of being told by a guide when to cast, where to drop the fly, when to strike, meanwhile listening to what the fish is doing and what it is going to do when the fisherman cannot even see it.

There comes a time when Joe is looking the other way—you see a big bone, a single old lunker cruising about 40 feet away. You make two false casts and then you shoot a lightning cast that lands like a feather in just the right spot about 5 feet ahead of it. Mr. Bone grabs the fly and rushes off; your reel screams. Joe turn. "Why, boss, you got one!"

"You bet I have, Joe, and I'll tell you how to net him." And when Mr. Bone is in the boat, all 8 pounds of him, it feels as if you'd made a hole-in-one.

I recall a windy, cold day with the tide high, the worst possible conditions for catching bonefish. A couple of gentlemen who had never bonefished before engaged a guide for a try on one of the bonefish flats. A fly rod was useless in this weather, and spinning with a wiggle jig proved equally unrewarding. In fact, it was impossible even to see a bonefish, though there was some evidence of "mudding" nearby. The guide said it was no use. "We must try bait. I'll go ashore and get a few crabs. I'll anchor the boat, and you gentlemen can stay here for fifteen or twenty minutes till I get back."

Anchored in the middle of the flat while their guide was a few hundred yards away looking for crabs, the two fishermen took advantage of the situation to improve their spinning technique with a little practice casting. After a few casts there was a sudden strike; the taut line whipped through the water at lightning speed, toward open water. Soon a 4½-pound bonefish was lying in the boat and two very excited fishermen were spanking the water on all sides with wiggle jigs. In a few moments another fish struck, and it too was landed—about the same size. By this time the guide hove into view on the way back to the boat with five or six soldier crabs wrapped in a piece of paper. Nothing was said until he reached the boat and saw the two fish lying on the bottom.

Joe's plywood skiff is perfect for bonefishing; he holds a worthy specimen to prove it.

"Man, how come these fish here in the boat?"

"Oh, we just tried a few casts when you were ashore and they took hold."

The guide just put his paper of crabs on the seat and said quietly, "Holy Communion."

It's the same sort of thing that plagues a golfer with a good caddy. I know, because in years past, I've had my periods of golf insanity. How often I have vowed to give up the game forever. How nearly I have come to wrapping my clubs around a tree and marching off the course once and for all. Then when everything looks completely hopeless (and your caddy is asleep), it happens: the 200-yard drive right to the green, the long 20-foot putt—the birdie two. The sun smiles again. You think of Arnold Palmer who usually got a three on the same hole. You join your friends in the locker room and make a date for another round a few days later. And so it goes with bonefish. Joe has located the bonefish; he has told you where they are, where to cast, when to cast, how to work your fly, and when to strike. How deflating— how frustrating . . . .

Some Bonefishermen

Perhaps I have been a little unfair to experienced bonefishermen in emphasizing the importance of the guide compared to the skills of the angler. There is no question that men who have had a lot of experience with bonefish will catch far more than a novice, guide or no guide. And there is no doubt that a man whose reactions are slow, who lacks accuracy in casting, and whose vision is poor is at a tremendous disadvantage.

The following are some necessary credentials for the man who would tackle the wily bonefish on his own. I give them in the order of their importance:

1. X-ray eyes that can penetrate water and detect these shadowy forms before they are aware of your presence.

2. An ability to read the telltale signs which bonefish make on the bottom, as well as color variations in the water caused by feeding fish.

3. Knowledge of the habits of bonefish and how they react to the movement of the tides, the direction and force of the winds, and the temperature of the air.

4. The ability to handle a fly in the wind; or a lure, if a spinning rod is preferred.

5. And lastly, the playing of the fish.

I asked Joe Brooks, who knows his way around a bonefish flat, for some tips on bonefishing and how he rated bonefish as compared to other sport fish, and this is what he wrote me (May 14, 1964):

It is almost impossible to try to compare the fights of different species. Where you catch them and on what tackle makes the difference. You can beat an Atlantic salmon at the rate of a pound a minute. Because of the long run it makes, you cannot do this with a bonefish. Leaping fish like the tarpon are spectacular, but all I can say to that is, "Thank goodness a bonefish doesn't jump."

You become attached to bonefish, get a kindly feeling toward them that makes you release each one you catch. You frown on anyone who keeps one, unless it is a fish for a mount, or perhaps a record fish.

The main thing to remember . . . is to be as quiet as you possibly can. I've seen them flush 100 feet away when the poling pole grated on coral. Make as few motions as possible. When they are close, cast horizontally so they have less chance of seeing the rod movement. Use flies that are right for the depth of water. Bonefish swim along the bottom. You seldom see them in the mid-water or near the surface. Use a small fly, say, on a no. 4 hook in water up to 12 inches deep, so the fly will not catch on the bottom. For water from a foot to 2 feet deep, use a no. 2 hook; and for water over 2 feet, use a still heavier hook, a 1/0.

A long, tapered leader helps. It should have a heavy butt

Joe Brooks, using flyfishing gear, keeps the bonefish's chin up to protect the line and leader from coral and shells on the bottom.

section, 25- or 30-pound test nylon, then taper down through 20, 15, 12, 10, to 8 or 6, depending on just how fine you want to go. A leader 12 to 14 feet long pays off, because the further away from the fly the line drops, the less noise there is to scare the fish. You need the heavy butt section to turn the leader over and present the fly in a the proper manner.

The strip method of retrieve works best. With this method you can make a very fast pull or a slow one. You can mix your bring-back up. You have the line and leader at your command throughout the retrieve and are ready at all times to strike, or to pick up your line for another cast.

Polaroid glasses are also important, because they cut the glare and allow you to spot the fish much more easily.

One last thing—be sure to look at the bottom, not stopping your gaze at the surface. Looking at the bottom you see the fish as it moves, while stopping your gaze at the surface you just don't see them.

You never forget the sight of that fleeting shadow in front of you, nor that fantastic flight across the flats. In fact you don't forget anything about bonefish, they stay with you for the rest of your angling life.

What angler has not heard of Lee Wulff? Perhaps more than any other person he has made fishing into a fine art. He has also perpetrated more ways of fooling fish than any one I know of. I have fished with Lee in Newfoundland, watching him take a 12-pound salmon with a 1½-ounce rod and one of his famous white Wulff flies. A man of many talents, he is unexcelled in sport-fishing photography, a skill that consumes me with envy. Wulff's movies of catching three 5-pound trout on one cast in Labrador, or his pictures of salmon fishing in Newfoundland are unforgettable.

Lee was one of the first fly-rod bonefisherman, and much of the credit for upgrading this method should go to him. I asked him for a comparison of fly fishing for salmon and bonefish, and particularly why the latter should take a fly at all since it is unusual to their diet. He wrote (May 21, 1964):

In comparing the attitudes of bonefish and salmon in regard to a fly presented to them it is necessary to consider the flylike food around them. With salmon there is a wide variety

The reward—a fine fish scooped from the water after a
"fantastic flight across the flats."

of insect life to which they have become accustomed as parr. These insects, as nymphs, swim the streams, and as flying insects hatch out and drift on the surface. In a salmon river, too, there are a great many terrestrial insects which fall in the water, like dragonflies, moths, bees, and many others. None of either category grows in or falls in the bonefish flats. The similarity for the two species lies in the crustaceans like the crawfish, shrimp, etc., of freshwater and their saltwater counterparts. It is these crustaceans, particularly the shrimp, that lie behind the bonefish fly. Flies for bonefish, therefore, need not have the variety nor do they offer the intriguing nuances that may be present in flies for salmon or trout.

Bonefish, however, are swift and predatory. If a fly does not frighten them when it lands they may, like most game fish, swiftly seize something that looks alive, looks good to eat, and looks, too, as if it might get away. I have had bonefish take a bass plug on the surface, although I know of nothing similar in their food range. We know too little of their possible flylike foods or their tastes to have covered the range of flies that will interest them. The developing of bonefish flies, as with dry flies for salmon, is still in its infancy and provides a great source of interest for the resourceful and inventive angler.

As there are all types of fishing so there are all types of fishermen, including those who want to know all the techniques of bonefishing in order to cope with the various imponderables of climate, temperature, water conditions, and the various factors which one has to diagnose in the pursuit of this wily and unpredictable fish. In going into these details there is wide scope for differences of opinion, and opinions differ greatly even among the experts. There are basic fundamentals to successful bonefishing, but no two experts will agree on all points.

I am reminded of an experiment conducted in Scotland by Lee Wulff and Jock Scott, who is also

Lee Wulff in 1947, with a bonefish caught on a fly rod at Grassy Key, Florida.

one of the world's best-known salmon fishermen. Lee is a proponent of the short rod and the lightest of tackle, while Jock Scott prefers a longer rod and heavier equipment. The two experts met by agreement on a Scottish river a few years ago. They covered the same pools under conditions which were as similar as could possibly be determined. There they tried out their different theories of fishing. Lee proved that he could catch and land salmon on a dry fly with a little rod and in fast playing time.

Then I thought of Sam Snead, whose exploits with bonefish reached a climax after he caught a 15-pounder that was described in *Time* magazine. Everyone who swings a golf club knows of Sam Snead, but few know that he can cast a fishing line as accurately as he can drive a golf ball. I thought there might be some subtle connection between the two, that co-ordination and timing might be the magic factors. I asked him about his 15-pound bonefish (which undoubtedly gave him more of a thrill than his holes-in-one), and he wrote me (May 12, 1964):

One of the most exciting things that ever happened to me was catching a bonefish weighing approximately 15 pounds using an Orvis spinning reel with a 6-pound test line opposite the residence of Mr. Bert Lyons in Bimini. This fish took me almost thirty-five minutes to land and he really seemed to know all the tricks! He was under the boat a couple of times where, in swapping ends with the fishing guide Willie Duncam, the fish was pulled over several times. I had to go over the boat with the rod, switching ends with the guide. I bowled him over and had to trade positions in the boat so as to keep the line from coming in contact with the boat. With that much pressure on the line it would have snapped in a second. It was a great thrill to catch this particular fish, and I was busier than a cat on a hot tin roof trying to keep it from getting tangled up with the small man-

Don McCarthy, head of the Fishing Information Bureau in the Bahamas, casts to a school of feeding fish.

grove shoots growing on the flats along with the ferns and conch shells. This fish made about three long runs, in addition to going back and forth under the boat; but when I brought him to the boat the last time, the guide put the net

Ray Ovington, outdoor writer, with a bonefish on the other
end of his spinning gear.

into the water and he seemed to move into it on his own. He seemed as beat as I was! There's an old saying, that when you land a bonefish, he usually has given his all. This one hardly moved once he was in the boat.

After looking the fish over, Willie said, "We go in now. I think we got something here!" I am almost positive that this fish weighed more than 15 pounds as it was out of the water for at least one and one-half hours before being weighed.

We couldn't find scales the moment we arrived at the dock and one of Mr. Lyons' "handy boys" was told to go down to the house on the beach and borrow a pair of scales. He made this trip after what seemed like hours and returned without them, saying he couldn't get into the house. To this Mr. Lyons replied, "Dammit, you should have broken the door down. Now, get those scales!" The boy again left and returned later with a pair which were small. With the fish's tail lying on the dock, he weighed in at 14½ pounds. We then started up the big boat and headed toward the official weigh-in station. We could only go about 10 mph because of the shallow water and very narrow channels. We finally got there and after another wait of fifteen or twenty minutes the scales were brought out. The fish was weighed in at an official 15 pounds.

I was serenaded loudly by the Bimini boys and had to join them in a march as this seemed to be the highlight of any fishing expedition for the season.

The fish now rests in my home. As I pass by it, I think of the wonderful fight he made to survive and the joy and pleasure which he gave me in catching him. Until someone beats this record, and I am sure it will come, I still think of him as the KING.

Ted Williams boats one with the help of his famous guide, Jimmy Albright.

Bonefish and Salmon

Nothing can be further from my thoughts than to draw conclusions between the virtues of two noble fish, the bonefish and the salmon. The differences are so great in all respects as to defy comparison. I have fished for the king of freshwater fishes enough to appreciate the delights of days spent on the bright rivers of the North; those experiences were thrilling indeed. But let us first consider the bonefish as it steals over the white Bahamas banks with the incoming tide.

Let me describe a typical experience. The bonefish is tailing, alone, and about 100 yards off. I approach quietly, trying at the same time to get the wind at my back because accurate casting against a strong wind is difficult. After stalking it for perhaps 75 yards I arrive within casting distance. Four false casts are necessary to get the right distance, but the final cast drops the fly, a Dunmore, just at the right spot. The fish swirls and strikes hard and an instant later is off on its mad dash for freedom. There is no way that a bonefish can be stopped on this initial run (even a small fish, 3 pounds or so, will usually take off 50 yards of line like lightning, and a 7- or 8-pounder will go 100 yards, or even more).

Incidentally, this matter of preliminary false-casting to get line out is important. False casts in the direction of the fish are fatal, as the swishing rod and whirling line in the air would spook the bonefish every time. False casts, preferably not more than two, must be made at right angles to the fish. But even at that the shadows of line or rod moving across the white bottom are often seen by the wary fish and cause it to spook. It is also important to have a few coils of loose line in the bottom of the boat (about

25 feet are enough), and these must be free of all objects on which the line could catch. There is no time to clear a line off your feet, or tackle box, or anchor rope, etc., in getting the line out before the final cast. This may sound easy, but in the hurry and excitement of reaching your target quickly, it is no small undertaking; when the wind is blowing it is practically impossible. That is the time to use the spinning rod. And one other point is important for successful bonefishing with a fly rod. In retrieving the fly that a bonefish is following, bring it in with slow, short jerks and when the fish gets close give it an extra speed-up—this will excite Mr. Bone and give him that extra urge to strike.

I have found that to stand still while this amount of line is being taken off the reel increases your chances greatly of losing the fish. Once a bonefish reaches the end of his run he will usually circle, and if your leader, under tension and by now on the bottom, comes in contact with one of the numerous small sea growths, it will break. The best course is to hold the rod as high as possible while reeling in, all the while pursuing the fish as fast as conditions permit. This may seem like an extraordinary way to

Ted Williams shows how it's done. After a couple of
false casts at right angles to the boat to get his line out, he
is ready to make his final cast a few feet ahead of a
feeding bonefish.

The cast is on its way. The line has straightened out
behind the boat, which is essential for accurate and proper
delivery of the fly.

Williams uses his left hand to give the fly the all-important jigging action.

Hooked and close to the boat, the bonefish is led gradually toward guide Jimmy Albright's net.

play a fish, but it pays off. Of twenty-four fish hooked on one occasion, eighteen were landed; of the ones that got away, two cut the leader on bottom growths, three were not substantially hooked, and the last one must have been a big one as it never did stop. This is not a typical experience, however. An angler will sometimes land six or seven straight without losing a single one; that number may be lost in rapid succession too. A fair average ratio of lost to landed fish is fifty-fifty.

Now let us consider the arguments pro and con of *Salmo salar* versus *Albula vulpes*. First, the environment. Surely those crisp, sparkling days on some northern river with the scent of pine in the air are something to dream about, but then so are soft sunny days on subtropic flats with dazzling clear water all about you and the radio reporting zero weather in the North. It's a draw.

The strike? Well, it is very different. Who has not cast and cast and cast over a dark pool in which a big salmon is resting? You've tried every pattern in the book, you've rested it, you've tried it wet and dry, but nothing doing. Then, perhaps, if you are lucky, the fish may suddenly take the same Black Dose that it has seen a hundred times before. How different Mr. Bone! You look and look and look until your eyes are unable to distinguish a fish from a piece of seaweed. And then that dark spot that you thought was a shadow starts to move. You think fast, but you haven't much time; the line must be out with a minimum of splash. The cast must be perfect, and if it is, wham! The verdict? It's a draw.

The battle? Your salmon rushes off in a wild run and leaps in the air again and again. After a while it settles down and sulks, recovering its strength for more runs and leaps. This may go on for as much as forty minutes or even more, but your salmon dies hard and often will escape even as the net or gaff closes in. But Mr. Bone, when the hook is set, rushes madly off, not 100 or 200 feet but 100 yards or more. It doesn't jump, but it does everything else except sulk. It doesn't take long; ten or fifteen minutes of perpetual motion and Mr. Bone comes to rest utterly exhausted. You can take him in with your hand. It's a tie vote.

Pound for pound the bonefish is a stronger fish than the Atlantic salmon. As to choice of flies, the salmon is a connoisseur while Mr. Bone is a roughneck; he prefers white or yellow or a combination of the two, but size is not very important.

So I've come to the answer of the question of *Salmo salar* versus *Albula vulpes*. When the warm days of June suggest a scent of pine and spruce and I become aware of the songs of nesting birds in the early morning hours of early summer; when I fancy a smell of smoked salmon or the pungent odor of citronella and tar, then I start to think of bright rivers and dark pools flanked by balsam and pine. And then I realize that nothing can take the place of quiet days spent on some remote salmon river in the North.

But when the leaves fall and chill winds presage a long dreary winter, can there be anything better than those white flats of the subtropics with their teeming marine life and sparkling clear, brilliant water? At times like these I think of swift shadows against the white sand and silver tails flashing in the sunlight.

And so, like blondes versus brunettes, you have an interesting choice—they're both wonderful, especially when conditions are favorable.

A Phantom Bonefish

I have often wondered why in the perennial tug of war between truth and fiction, fiction usually gets the upper hand. When it comes to fishing, I observe how the large fish which escapes the net seems to grow in weight each passing year. Yet, in articles about fishing, it is pleasant and exciting to live again with the angler those battles with mighty fish which have happy endings. On the other hand, how disillusioning and frustrating if the fish finally escapes and leaves *Homo sapiens* holding, instead of a trophy, a broken line!

I am trying hard to be factual and cling to the straight and narrow path of truth; and this has not been difficult to do, as I have no need to exaggerate. Bonefish, to my mind, present more variety of antics, produce more problems for the angler, create more frustrations in catching them, and cost more money per pound to angle for them than any other fish that swims, except possibly salmon. Having caught upwards of 2,000 or more in my winters spent in the Bahamas and other bonefish hangouts, I have no need to call upon my imagination in telling of their prowess.

But in every fisherman's life, there come occasionally certain fishing experiences so different from the normal, so unusual, so hard to believe, that the pure unvarnished truth about such catches transcends anything that an author could embellish as fiction.

The following is a true account, and it is my contribution to the fact that sometimes, in every fisherman's experience, truth is indeed stranger than fiction.

On the northern tip of Eleuthera Island in the Bahamas, there is a tiny settlement known as the Current. About 3 miles from this settlement there are two brackish ponds about 100 or more acres in size, surrounded by scrub growth and an occasional banana farm. A road connects the Current with another settlement known as the Bluff; and a spur from this road passes near the ponds. These ponds have no names. They are very shallow except for occasional holes of undetermined depth. No one knows how the ponds got there—some say a flood a century or so ago deluged the area, and when the water receded it left these ponds in the depressions. There are no connections between the ponds and the nearby ocean, though some say there is underground seepage between them and the salt water. There does seem some evidence of this, as there is a slight rise and fall of tide which is accentuated by rainfall from time to time. Giant bonefish are supposed to inhabit the ponds, having supposedly been trapped by the flooding sea during some hurricane, beyond the memory of the natives who live nearby. This myth of giant bonefish has grown up over the years like the Loch Ness monster in Scotland; but no one has ever caught a bonefish in these unnamed ponds and no one has ever claimed to have actually seen one, though bonefish tails have been sometimes reported. The only visitors to these ponds are bird-hunters who bang away at coots and ducks from the shore.

Harbour Island is a small resort about ten miles or so away. I have a winter hideout there which I use as a bonefishing headquarters. One of my neighbors, and a good friend, is Paul Tappan—a retired yachtsman who has a well-developed pioneering spirit and a yen to go to out-of-the-way places like Caicos Island, Mayaguana, etc. For two years Paul had been intrigued by the stories about the ponds and had tried to get me to go there and put an end, once and for all, to the uncertainties of the bonefish myth.

So, one March, we enlisted the cooperation of Bonefish Joe. Paul contributed a tiny aluminum skiff used as a tender for his yacht; and we hired Dubie Eldon, a native of the Current who had a car, for taxi service between the settlements. One of our Bahaman friends dug us some mollie crabs for bait. I had not used bait for bonefish for several years— only flies and jigs—but our attitude toward this proj-

Bonefish Joe packs our skiff to the pond of the phantoms.

ect was more like an investigation in the interests of science than a trip for sport.

Bonefish Joe's boat took us across the harbor to Eleuthera Island, where we were met by Dubie. We put Paul's skiff on top of Dubie's car and proceeded to drive the 10 miles to one of the ponds. On arrival, Joe grabbed the boat and proceeded, unaided, to put it on his head. He marched off over slippery coral rock and mud to the water's edge. Since the boat could with difficulty hold only two men of ordinary size (Joe weighs over 200 pounds and, when guiding for bonefish, always stands up), I gazed at the quicksand and mud bottom with a dubious eye and suggested that Paul make the first assault on *Albula vulpes.*

"Oh, no," he said. "You are the expert. You should make the first try."

"Oh, no," I said. "This is a Tappan idea. You are the leader of Operation Precarious."

"Well, we'll draw," he said, pulling out a Bahama ten-cent piece, which has two wicked-looking bonefish on the tail side, "You call," he said. "Queen Elizabeth or bonefish."

"Queen Elizabeth," I said.

"Bonefish," said Paul, without enthusiasm. "Guess it's my turn first."

He said this rather sadly, I thought.

"I'll go for half an hour; then it's your turn."

Dubie and I watched them as they embarked, and we waited with restrained thinking for their return. As they reached shore, Paul said, "How can one fish in mud?"

"You're still living," I replied. "Be grateful!"

"Your turn," he answered, with what I suspected was a glint in his eye. "We saw nothing," he said. "How could we? Six inches down, and it was the color of *cafe au lait*. I didn't know where to cast," he said ruefully.

This gave me a tip. "I'll put a white weighted fly on my spinning rod," I said. A bonefish, unless blind, could probably see it if not more than 3 feet away.

So we started out along the shore, Joe watching the shallows, and I blind-casting the more opaque and deeper water. A half hour of barren results followed. No life was apparent except a few flocks of coots and the swirl of a houndfish we had caught napping.

We were on the opposite side of the pond, about 30 feet from shore, when suddenly Joe froze and said breathlessly, "Holy Communion! Look about 8 feet to your left. Do you see what I sees?"

I looked; and there facing me was a large bone-fish—motionless, and looking at me with large, black, evil-looking eyes. And behind it was a boy (or girl) friend, even larger.

"Cast quick," said Joe.

Now, you devotees of the spinning rod, how do you cast 8 feet accurately with a large bonefish looking at you? I made a mess of it. "Cast again," said Joe, "and get it in front of him."

To make an 8-foot cast under tension is, to me, impossible to do accurately. Another dismal failure! The bonefish stared on. Perhaps it had never seen a boat before, much less a wild man casting at him.

"Move away, Joe; give me room. I don't dare raise my arm."

"Can't," said Joe. "He'd spook."

Just then the bonefish moved slowly to one side, perhaps 15 feet off, accompanied by its aide-de-camp. This gave me the room I needed, and I dropped the weighted fly right in front of him. It immediately became invisible in the murky water. I started to jig it—something caught.

"I'm stuck on the bottom, Joe."

"Reel in gently," Joe said.

"Still stuck," I wailed.

"No, Boss, I see dat fly in his mouth. Give him some more pressure."

I tightened up and, to my amazement, Mr. Bone started to come toward the boat.

"I'm going to net him," Joe whispered hoarsely.

"Hold the net still in the water, Joe," I said, "and I'll try and guide him into it. This fish must be sick, or else he has no more interest in life."

Joe held out the net, but to no avail; so I struck. Then all hell broke loose. The pond beside us exploded. That bonefish had discovered finally that he was hooked. Perhaps the hook had penetrated to a sensitive part of his mouth. At any rate, he took off for the center of the pond—not with the lightning speed of a 4- or 5-pound bonefish, but with the power and drive of a bulldozer. Fortunately, I had on a new 8-pound-test Stren line, and I put on all the drag I dared. But it made no difference. The line moved out slowly but inexorably.

"Tighten the drag!" yelled Joe.

"I can't, I can't! I don't dare!" I shouted back. "Follow him, Joe, for Pete's sake! My line is getting low!"

I looked at the reel, and only a pitiful amount remained on the core—perhaps only 20 yards of the 200-yard capacity.

I shall never forget that run. It seemed interminable; but finally it slowed down and stopped.

"He's found a deep hole," I thought, "and will rest."

"Paddle after him, Joe!" I shouted. "Help me regain some line for the next run."

"No, sir," replied Joe. "I see branches sticking up out dere and trouble. If I move from here you'll lose dat fish, sure."

"All right, I'll stay here."

I could make no headway by reeling; but by slowly pumping a couple of yards at a time I started to retrieve line. Ten yards—20 yards—30 yards—then a halt. I could get no more. Mr. Bonefish then took a sidewise course, diagonally across us, and this was fortunate; because I could, by pressure, influence him to veer toward us.

How long this went on I have no idea—perhaps ten, perhaps twenty, maybe thirty minutes. It seemed ages. But I finally gained line and commenced to breathe easier. There were other halts and other runs, but the fish's tail never came to the surface, which would have indicated a sign of weakness. Finally it neared the boat, and the problem of netting it confronted us.

"He's not ready yet," whispered Joe. But clearly most of its fight was gone; and by leading it round and round the little skiff in ever smaller circles, I brought it within netting distance.

"Keep the net under water and motionless, Joe; and if you muff him, I'll never speak to you again."

Once or twice it came very close to the waiting net, but turned aside at the last minute. But eventually it made it, and Joe lifted the utterly exhausted fish into the boat. With trembling hands I reached for the scales. It read 9¼ pounds.

After a while, I said, "What about that other fish, Joe, which looked even larger?"

Now, as I have said earlier, Joe's enthusiasm for fishing is supreme. He never wants to quit. "Just one more fish," he often says. "We got de time for a look at de flat on de way back." This characteristic of Joe makes his answer to my question all the more amazing. After a long pause he said, "Boss, I don't want to catch that other one. Then people will say we done caught de last two and dere ain't no more. Isn't it better to leave dem somethin' to talk about? Besides," he said, with a touch of softness, I thought, "dat other fish was his buddy."

When we got back to Paul and Dubie, they gazed in awe at our phantom bonefish; and Dubie said simply, "Well, now we know the truth."

A phantom bonefish—and its big brother is still there.

How, all through the years, could it be that no one
before had ever caught a bonefish in the pond? Those
ponds are still there, and so is that other fellow—the
bonefish's buddy. Are there other bonefish there too?
Are there any small ones? Do they have underground
access to the ocean? What about the second pond
that we never tried? Are these monsters there too?
And if so, how old are they? These are still interesting projects for one to explore—maybe next winter.

Bonefishing Areas

Where are bonefish found? Generally there is little sense in fishing for bonefish in the surf or by trolling, or in fact in fishing for them in waters more than 4 feet deep. Bonefish the world over feed on flats or in shallows where the bottom is either of sand or marl or grassy. They feed in with the tide and then rest for a period (preferably in the mangroves if they can find any). When the tide turns they feed out in somewhat deeper waters, where they also rest. While bonefish can be caught on the ebb tide as well as on the flood tide, the best time is the last hour of the ebb and the first two hours of the flood tide.

There is no best season for catching bonefish. They are always there, winter and summer, but what is important and what is seasonable are the weather and temperatures. Water temperature is all-important. When it is below 70° F. bonefish definitely become harder to catch, and at 60° they seem to disappear entirely. When the shallow water is 60°, nearby deeper water is much warmer. A flat warmed by the hot sun is apt to teem with hundreds of bonefish. That night if the temperature drops and a wind comes up, as it frequently does in the wintertime, the same flat could be empty of bonefish the following day. Air temperature is only important as it affects the water temperature and the disposition of the angler.

It is safe to say that the warmer the water the better the bonefishing. I would also feel safe in saying that this effect of the weather on bonefishing is worldwide and that there is no "season" for bonefish.

While most bonefishing is done in parts of the Bahamas and along the Florida Keys, there are many other areas throughout the world where one can find excellent bonefishing. In fact, I would wager that wherever there are warm-water flats in tropics and semitropic climates there will be bonefish waiting for action.

I am often asked, "Where does one go for good bonefishing?" This is easy to answer if one is interested in the Florida Keys, the coastal waters of Central America, and the Caribbean area, including the Bahamas. Worldwide this general area is the mecca of sport fishing for bonefish. It was in the Florida Keys that sport fishing for bonefish was first discov-

A Bahamas out-island from the air, showing ocean and beach on the right and bonefish flats on the left.

ered, and the area is a playground for tourists and anglers. Fishing camps are abundant, and cruising waters are so convenient that these fish are challenging the popularity of such great saltwater fishes as sailfish, marlin, and tarpon.

Even though the distribution of bonefish is worldwide, universal bonefishing for sport is in its infancy. Three important ingredients are necessary for a bonefishing paradise:

1. The area must be in tropic waters where there are great stretches of sand, marl, or grass flats.

2. There should be reasonably appropriate accommodations where one can stay and where there are

facilities, such as suitable boats and guides familiar with specific flats.

3. The area should not be far removed from the mainstream of tourism or remote from adequate transportation facilities.

When one considers these requirements, there are relatively few places right now which can qualify. Indeed, I have met and talked with sportsmen in many lands—Chile, Scotland, Scandinavia, India, Argentina, and Europe—who are anglers of experience who have actually never heard of bonefish or who have only the vaguest of notions about them.

This situation will not exist long. As bonefishing becomes better known and new habitat areas are discovered and made convenient, its popularity will increase just as it has increased in the Caribbean area.

Bonefish are not a rare or unknown species. Throughout the warm seas they are well known by native folk, but more edible fish are abundant and are so easy to catch that the natives do not bother with bonefishing. Such bonefish as are caught or netted are taken largely by accident. (There are, however, exceptions to this. Those that are caught in nets, as in Hawaii and doubtless elsewhere, bring good prices as marlin bait.) While there are a diversity of lures and fishing techniques in vogue in different parts of the world, bonefish are bonefish the world over and will respond to all lures and baits mentioned in this book.

Here are a few localities where bonefishing is well established:

Bermuda: For some years the world's record bonefish came from the Bermuda flats. There are many special places there which are particularly popular: Pompano and Whale Bay, for example, and the beaches at Shelley. One can use a fly rod at these places. At other spots where bonefish are plentiful the water is deeper and bait or spinning lures are more productive.

Although bonefish can be caught all year round in Bermuda the best season is from April to December. For further information, the Bermuda Trade Development Board at Hamilton is very cooperative in giving fishing advice and in suggesting places to stay. Write Pete Perinchief, director of the Fishing Information Bureau.

Unfortunately the *Florida Keys* are the only area in the United States where one can find bonefish, but wherever there are flats from Miami to Key West, one can get excellent bonefishing with good accommodations and good guides. Also the bonefish in these waters average somewhat larger than the bonefish in other areas. This is probably due to the proximity of the warm Gulf Stream where there is an abundance of food.

Across the Gulf Stream in the *Bahamas* there are 750 miles of countless bonefish flats, all the way from Walkers Key south to the Caicos and Grand Turk Islands. The only trouble in fishing these outlying areas is that one needs to have a cabin cruiser to live on and one equipped with a small skiff or two for fishing the flats. There are, however, many places throughout the Bahamas where one can find good accommodations and where suitable arrangements can be made for bonefishing. The Bahama Tourist Bureau in Nassau has a list of these places: Deepwater Key at Grand Bahama, the owner of which is

Gil Drake; Chub Key at the extreme southern end of the Berry Islands; the new development on Great Harbor Key on the northern end of the Berrys; the Peace and Plenty Club, Georgetown; Great Exhuma, and so on, to mention just a few of the better-known.

A good cruise boat is the yacht *Hope*, based at West End, Bahamas; its address is Yacht *Hope*, West End Yacht Club, Bahamas. The captain, Glen Tatum, operates fishing cruises from November 1 to June 15.

With a comfortable yacht such as the *Hope*, which can accommodate six anglers (or three couples), one

The yacht Hope, *a fine one for bonefishing cruises.*

can cruise for a week or more and never see another soul or even another boat, much less another fisherman. In such isolation it is exciting to discover new flats and explore tropical keys always with the feeling that you may be fishing a spot seldom or maybe never fished before. In fishing such out-of-the-way places we found the bonefish tame and cooperative but just as full of fight when hooked as anywhere else. The yacht's maneuverability makes each day a fresh adventure.

In the *U. S. Virgin Islands* the southern coast of St. Croix with its shallow reefs is best, especially Krause Lagoon. At St. John, Leinster Bay on the northern coast and Reef and Fish bays on the southern coast have bonefish, but they are rare at St. Thomas.

In the *British Virgin Islands* there is an island known as Beef Key. It is just off the northern tip of Tortola. I have been advised that there are flats around Beef Key where the bonefishing is fabulous, and they are seldom fished except by some stray tourist or angler with a well-developed pioneering spirit. Unfortunately there is no place to stay on Beef Key, unless one is on a yacht. There are accommodations of a sort on nearby Tortola.

The southern coast of Anegada in the British Virgin Islands should have bonefish because of the extensive sand and coral shallows.

Hawaii has some excellent bonefishing waters, and until two years ago the world's record fish, 18 pounds, was caught there. Unfortunately, a lot of netting is done in Hawaii, and it is pretty difficult for bonefish to prosper where the netting of them is extensive.

Joe Brooks has investigated bonefishing in *East African* waters and writes in his book *A World of Fishing:*

We heard stories of bonefish up to 25 pounds but though we searched diligently we found none. To prove, however, that bonefish do live in the area Jack deSantos sent word to some commercial fishermen and they brought in four bonefish and sent them to me. They were quite small, well under 4 pounds, and as it happened they were taken in deep water around the reefs.

For some reason the bonefish in this area seem to stay in the deep, apparently not feeding in the shallows as they do in the Atlantic Ocean and therefore not providing the same sport for light tackle anglers.

However, if they are ever discovered feeding in shallow waters anywhere in the Indian Ocean they will become the popular game fish that they are in the United States.

The world's record catch was made in an area where bonefish are not caught for sport. In a letter to me (July 31, 1964) Brian W. Batchelor described the bonefishing situation that exists in *South African* waters:

Yes, it was a great thrill to land the world's largest bonefish recorded up to now.

But I must be honest with you and your readers. You must understand that in this neck of the beaches we do not fish for bonefish as such. The bonefish is not greatly regarded here because he is usually taken on tackle on which we are hoping to land more powerful fish. Such fish would be Carangid, Sciaenids, Serranids, and Scomberomorids, as well as the odd sharks and rays. The more interesting specimens of the above genera may range from 20 pounds to 100 pounds in weight; the sharks and rays will take similar baits and may go up to several hundred pounds in weight.

Obviously our tackle must be adequate, and we may have

to haul these fellows out from rocky situations. These fish are caught from a shore stance, and we fish straight into an ocean which stretches from here to Australia. There are no offshore islands or reefs to break the violence of the surf. So stout tackle prevails. For bait-fishing 30-pound B.S. nylon monofilament is considered minimum, and a 6-ounce pyramid sinker is standard to hold the bait out in the waves. When lures are judged necessary they will range from 4½ to 6 ounces. Rods for handling these are seldom less than 11½ feet long.

I have caught numerous bonefish up to 10 pounds, and very gamy fish they have always been, but as above described, they have not really had a chance. Now my impression of American fishing for this fish is that they are taken with much stealth and fine tackle in calm shallows of bays and inlets.

So it is not possible for me to be lyrical about the actual capturing of this fish. The thrill came later when I discovered that it was a world record, although I was reasonably sure that the local record had been surpassed by my fish.

As stated previously, bonefish inhabit all tropic waters where there are shallow flats and where they can find their food in abundance, but in most of the areas outside of the eastern shores of Central America, the Florida Keys, and the Bahamas, bonefish are hardly known and not considered a sporting fish. The state of Quintana Roo in *Mexico* and the eastern-shore flats of *Honduras* and *British Honduras* are fabulous areas for bonefish, but are entirely overlooked except in a few choice spots. One of these spots is the Boca Paila camp at Tulum in Quintana Roo, Mexico. This can be reached via Mérida or Cozumel Island, where the owner, Antonio Gonzales, can take you over in his private plane to his camp. It's a twenty-minute flight from Cozumel. Bonefish are here by the thousands, though they are small, averaging 2 to 3 pounds. A 5- or 6-pounder would be a big one. Another place is the Pez Maya fishing camp, also in Quintana Roo, with deserted Mayan ruins all about. Bookings are handled by World Wide Sportsman's Inc. of Islamorada, Florida. Another camp where fishing is fabulous, not only for bonefish but also for permit and tarpon in season, is the Turneffe Island Lodge at Belize in British Honduras. This camp was formerly owned by Vic Borothy, whose camp at the Isle of Pines, Cuba, was probably the number-one camp anywhere until Castro took it over. This camp is 25 miles east of Belize, which has an air service with Miami, TAM Airlines. Another very interesting camp near Belize is the Keller Caribbean Sport Lodge. Reservations here can be made by Leigh Perkins, president of the Charles F. Orvis Co., Manchester, Vermont. I have never been there, but reportedly the bonefishing is fabulous. The camp is situated on the bank of the Belize River, a couple of miles from the sea. The camp also has a houseboat accommodating one to four people with a crew of four, a skipper and highly expert guides, for houseboat fishing trips along the coastal keys.

It is sad to leave Cuba and the Isle of Pines out of this book, as it is probably the best area of all for shallow-water fishing. Perhaps the day will come when it will be possible for foreigners again to fish its teeming waters for bonefish, permit, and tarpon.

The *Cayman Islands* just west of Jamaica are beautiful, and all three of them have excellent accommodations, but for bonefishing, Little Cayman Island is by far the best place. These islands can be reached through the tourist bureau in Miami.

Bonefishing in remote areas of the world is not practical yet for most bonefish enthusiasts. However, pioneers with a yen for adventure can be well advised by Leigh Perkins of the Orvis Co. It's always best, however, to also seek the counsel of a fisherman who has fished these out-of-the-way places. In my travels to foreign lands I have always tried to ask questions about the bonefish and the fishing for it, but where the natives speak English they do not know it by that name, and I cannot describe it with any degree of assurance that they know what I'm talking about.

I did have one experience that has an exception to this, on Castaway Island in the Fijis in 1971. There were a few vacationing Australians there and I got into conversation with a rugged scuba diver who had been exploring the magnificent Barrier Reef and speared a certain number of black fish. I asked him if he knew anything about bonefish and he said, "It's strange that you should ask me that, because this very morning at the low tide, I was passing a shallow flat and saw a great quantity of silver fish, a foot or two long, feeding on the sand bottom with their tails waving above the surface. As I approached them, they suddenly, with a great explosion of water, disappeared. I've been reading a book about bonefishing someone in the States sent me, and I wondered if they actually were the fish I had been reading about." I asked him if the name of the author was by any chance Babson, and he said "Yes, that's it"—for the book was the first edition of this one. I said, "That's me, and they were bonefish that you saw." He put down his cocktail said, "The hell you say."

Unfortunately, we were scheduled to take our plane eastward in the morning—and it was hard to leave those bonefish in their splendid isolation.

Bonefish Life Cycle and Structure

I am amazed when I consider the diversity of life cycles of the creatures that live in the sea, and of the miracles which have taken place beneath the water. Think of the mollusks, for example—those billions of animals that fashion shells of every hue and intricate design to serve as their protective homes. Millions of tons of lime are extracted from the ocean for this purpose by the tiny invertebrates. Rachel Carson relates in *The Sea Around Us* that almost all known chemical elements are found in the ocean, and a cubic mile of the sea contains $12 million worth of gold.

While vast information is available on life in the ocean, countless mysteries are still unsolved, and baffling questions are still to be answered.

It is incomprehensible that an eel born in the Sargasso Sea southeast of Bermuda will find its way over a year later as a tiny, flat, transparent larva to the mouth of some river or stream where it ascends the fresh water and remains from five to twenty years, only to return eventually to its breeding ground to reproduce and die.

Or take the Atlantic salmon, bred in our northern rivers, where it stays for three years and then seeks the ocean, eventually returning, a year to nine years later, to the river of its birth. Where do salmon go in winter? Some say the Continental Shelf; others suggest they slip under the polar ice cap. The subject is still under investigation.

But these examples of life cycles are no stranger than that of bonefish. Dr. Lavett Smith of the American Museum of Natural History in New York tells me that we know less about bonefish than most of our other fishes. This apparent oversight is now being actively remedied, however, and studies are underway at various laboratories, such as those at Bimini in the Bahamas and the International Oceanographic Foundation at Miami.

Dr. Smith reports that there is considerable evidence that bonefish lay eggs that float. When favorable conditions are found, related either to heat or light, a rapid transformation takes place in the development of the larvae, which then undergo an extraordinary metamorphosis to assume the physical characteristics of the future adult. Where these small bonefish go in their formative period is still a mystery, probably "just beyond the surf zone." I believe this may be so, because I have occasionally caught bonefish hardly 6 inches in length while surfcasting for pompano. Yet of the more than 2,000 bonefish I have caught in harbors and in protected shallows and flats, not one has been smaller than 13 or 14 inches, weighing approximately a pound. Few if any of the young appear to inhabit the flats and shallows.

Considerable study has been done on grouper fish in the laboratory at Bimini, and it has been established that several varieties of groupers in that area are born as females; after five years their reproductive organs undergo complete change and they become males for the final three to five years of life. Dr. Smith feels that it is quite possible that this extraordinary characteristic also applies to bonefish. (This may account for the fact that I have never found any roe in any bonefish I have examined. And I might indicate that when bonefish get large enough to leave their point of origin to enter the harbors and flats they are all males, though this is hard to believe.)

Mrs. Phyllis Cahn at the American Museum is studying the ability of fish to hear airborne sounds. I asked her about auditory senses of bonefish, and she advised that they could hear only about 5 percent of airborne sounds. On the other hand, sounds transmitted directly through the water, such as by an oar hitting a boat or the boat scraping on sand, could be detected for some distance.

I know that the sudden start of an outboard motor as much as 100 yards away will often spook a nearby school of bonefish. I also believe that a reel with a strong click will transmit the sound vibrations down the line, which, when entering the water, will frighten any bonefish nearby.

Many years ago I spent a day with Dr. William Beebe at his laboratory camp on Nonsuch Island in Bermuda. One of his assistants, Miss Gloria Hollister, had been working with a night light to collect specimens of small fish in order to write a paper on the caudal skeleton of small fishes in the Bermuda area. On one of these nightly vigils, Miss Hollister discovered what turned out to be the first larva of a bonefish ever found. Her discovery made a fascinating story, and I quote the following from her account in the *Bulletin of the New York Zoological Society* (May-June 1936). The illustration of bonefish development is adapted from a drawing by George Swanson which appeared in the same issue.

116

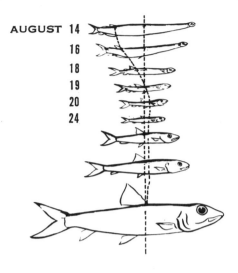

AUGUST 14
16
18
19
20
24

No sooner had I returned to my night-light vigil than a small silver dot was reflected by the light. This I followed for some time, knowing that it was the eye of a fish but not knowing what kind of fish it enlightened. Like the eel that had just been caught, it, too, was out of reach. But in a few minutes it was attracted nearer the center of the beam of light and then I saw a narrow, white, ribbon-like body trailing behind the glistening eye. It was a young of the world-known bone-fish, or *Albula vulpes.* Many have been caught in this stage when they resemble the young of certain eels and look not at all like their parents. At this particular time I happened to be working out the developing of the skeleton of the *Albula* from the very young to the adult. Hoping that this one would be an intermediate stage in our collection, I decided to catch it. After submerging the hand net and slowly raising its rim around the fish, I held it there for a long time and watched this delicate spark of life. To lift the fish out of water would snuff out its life in a few seconds! As I watched it swimming around within the net I remembered the many that had come in our seine and surface nets and their short survival after being pulled in. Almost without thinking I slipped a small glass dish into the water within the net and gradually raised it around the fish. This was done without touching or shocking the fish by lifting it out of water even for a second. The dish with the fish was then submerged in a 2-gallon tank. Before leaving that evening the fish's length, shape, and general description were jotted down. The next morning on the way to the boathouse I prepared a vial of preservative in which to keep the little *Albula* for study. Much to my surprise the fish was as lively as when captured the night before. I had even left it without an air supply.

Not dreaming that the *Albula* would live over the second night and wanting to study it in the laboratory, I again dipped it up in a small pint dish. Here it continued to live for two days without air supply, food, or change of water. I was amazed to see during this time how rapidly it was changing. It then dawned upon me that this larval *Albula* should be given the best possible conditions. It was again placed in a 2 gallon aquarium with a good supply of air and food, which consisted of plankton dipped up each evening from under the night-light. The young Albula was 2¼ inches long when it was caught on August 14. It was pure white and transparent and its small dorsal fin was way aft in position. According to daily measurements the fish grew more rapidly during the first four days; in fact, growth was less and less rapid on each successive day. Contrary to most fishes the growth in our living *Albula* was day by day decreasing in length. During the first forty-eight hours it decreased more than ½ inch and during the following forty-eight hours it shortened about ¼ inch. During the next four days the decrease in length was still less, being only a fraction of an inch. During ten days this living *Albula* larva changed completely before our eyes. It grew shorter and shorter, more round, more compact, more opaque, and the dorsal fin developed from an insignificant one, in a posterior position, to a prominent fin in the center of the body. The little fish began to acquire color, which first showed as dusky blotches mixed with yellow which in turn changed to dusky silver. When our *Albula* had decreased in length to about 1 inch, or a little more than one-third of its length when caught, it was a perfect miniature of its 3 foot parent. It was identical in general form, positions of the fins, proportion of the body, and hint of color.

Our living *Albula* decreased in ten days from 2¹/₄ inches to less than 1 inch, which gives us a hint of the amazing rapidity of transformation in this species of fish. From a one inch miniature-adult the *Albula* grows longer and larger; but we do not, as yet, know the length of time this takes. After having grown by shrinking for ten days our living *Albula* was attacked by fin fungus and in order to keep it for record and study it was preserved in spirits.

This is believed to be the first *Albula vulpes* to be reared from the leptocephalus to the young-adult form. It gives us a clue to the possibility of filling in the many gaps in the life histories of fishes.

It must be remembered, of course, that this interesting paper of Miss Hollister's was written several decades ago. Since that time many studies have been made of the life cycle of bonefish in many parts of the world, and while much mystery has been cleared up there are still some unsolved problems; for instance, where and how the egg develops into the gelatinlike larva are still unknown. Thanks to Miss Hollister we know that the larval form disappears during an eight-to-ten-day period, and it is replaced by a miniature adult bonefish.

Since her discovery on Nonsuch Island, Miss Hollister and other scientists have described the unusual metamorphosis and growth of larval bonefish; yet little or no mention has been made by them of the growth of the juveniles following metamorphosis.

In the course of gathering age-length data on young northern kingfish at Mercers Island in Great South Bay, New York, during the early summer and fall of 1962 more than a hundred juvenile bonefish were unexpectedly collected. Where did they come from? The only explanation is that they came through larval drift and inshore migration of metamorphosing leptocephali into an environment suitable for transformation.

More astonishing than the above was the catch of a 24-inch adult bonefish in a pound net in 1948 in Chesapeake Bay. Staff biologists at the Bureau of Marine Fisheries have never seen or collected a bonefish from Long Island waters in more than ten years of field study. Elizabeth C. Alexander (1961) stated that bonefish larvae were taken by plankton nets offshore where bottom depths, even near the shore, may reach four thousand meters, but the metamorphosing stages were captured by dip nets in shallow bay areas. From this it was assumed that spawning takes place either offshore or in areas where currents would take the eggs offshore.

Although bonefish may spawn the year round in the West Indies, Donald S. Erdman, curator of mollusks, Institute of Marine Biology at the University of Puerto Rico, caught larvae at Puerto Rico every month except July, and he found ripe bonefish only during the months of November through January. Erdman estimated a possible floating stage of development from five to six months. This could provide ample time for larvae from the West Indies, Florida, or Bermuda to arrive off Long Island by late July or early August.

According to the Smithsonian Miscellaneous Collections, bonefish are found in almost every tropical sea but are not confined to such. Individual fish sometimes extend their wanderings quite beyond the tropic zone, occasionally roaming northward as far as Massachusetts. Notwithstanding the above, *Albula vulpes* is a shore fish and seeks its food close to the shore or on muddy or sandy flats.

What do bonefish eat? I have opened a number of stomachs but never seemed to find anything but sand and bits of shells. However, Dr. Erdman has gone into this subject in detail, and I am indebted to him for supplying recent data.

Dr. Erdman found in his studies in 1960 that over 50 percent of all food consumed by a large group of bonefish called *macaco* in Puerto Rican waters was mollusk in origin. Fifty-six bonefish weighing between ¾ pound and 10¼ pounds were individually examined during the study. The majority of the fish were caught by means of gill nets and seines, usually on moonless nights. All fish were collected in the reef areas of La Parguera on the southeast coast of Puerto Rico. The whole digestive tract was removed, and the contents of both stomach and intestines were completely examined. The different types of food—mollusks, crustaceans, fishes, worms, etc.—were separated, their percentage by volume estimated, and the mollusks' species were determined wherever possible. Clams and snails made up over half of the bonefish's diet and were mostly in shell pieces and small fragments. Fragmentation probably resulted from the crushing action of the strong pharyngeal teeth of the bonefish during feeding. Subsequently, many other similar tests were made, and in all 303 bonefish were examined.

There is a correlation between the fish's food and the structural means for assimilating it. The dentition as a whole is quite peculiar—unlike that of any other animal. The bony roof of the mouth is closed in by the juxtaposition of the parasphenoid pterygoid bones and covered by rounded molar teeth like pearly beads; the roof of the mouth has opposed teeth

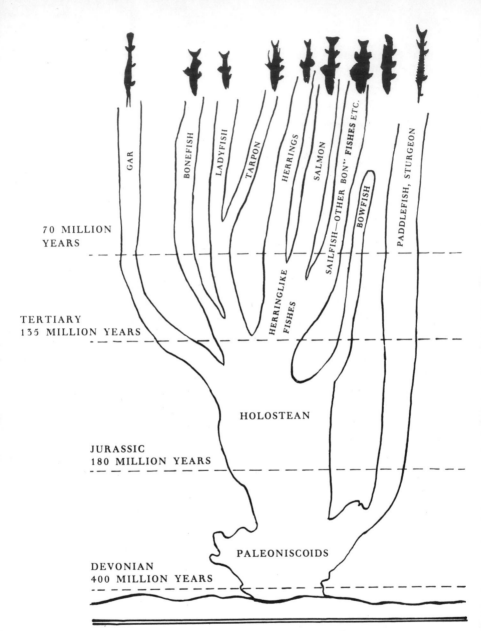

GAR
BONEFISH
LADYFISH
TARPON
HERRINGS
SALMON
SAILFISH—OTHER BONY FISHES ETC.
BOWFISH
PADDLEFISH, STURGEON

70 MILLION
YEARS

TERTIARY
135 MILLION YEARS

HERRINGLIKE
FISHES

HOLOSTEAN

JURASSIC
180 MILLION YEARS

PALEONISCOIDS

DEVONIAN
400 MILLION YEARS

Family Tree of Bonefish

so that the fish is well provided with the means for crushing the shells that it takes. Externally there is provision for finding and rooting them up in the projecting conical snout which is so prominent as to have suggested one of its early names, *Conorhynchus,* or "cornsnout."

The accompanying pie diagram illustrates the food types ingested. The most prevalent food item was a small white clam about ½ inch in diameter known as *Codakia costata.*

Dr. Erdman has indicated that bonefish are most abundant on the flats in May but that leptocephalus larvae were collected in every month of the year except July. These were most abundant from March to May and scarcest in October and November.

How does the unusual bonefish relate to the great order of fishes past and present? Richard Lund, graduate student at Columbia University and associated with the American Museum of Natural History, has specialized in the early history of *Albula vulpes.* His research reveals that it is estimated that the closest ancestors of *Albula vulpes* probably lived 130 million years ago, and the bonefish is one of the few fishes which can boast a family history of this duration.

Ancestors of all bony fishes are classified as Paleoniscoids. They date back 350 million years, and of this group only two species remain: the sturgeon and the paddlefish. All others are extinct.

From this group are descended the Holosteans, which inhabited the waters of the earth about 200 million years ago. Of these only two species remain: the gar and bowfin.

Descended from the Holosteans are the Teleosts, which developed some 135 million years ago. Two

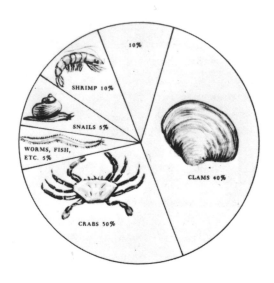

10%

SHRIMP 10%

SNAILS 5%

WORMS, FISH,
ETC. 5%

CLAMS 40%

CRABS 50%

branches developed from them, one being the Albulidae, of which our bonefish, ladyfish, and tarpon are the only remaining members. (For years *Albula vulpes* was called ladyfish, and it still is in some localities, but it is a misnomer. The ladyfish, while related, is of an entirely different genus.) But other branches, such as herring and salmon, were the progenitors of most of our present-day fishes and came along later, as the tree shows.

This family tree points up the fact that *Albula vulpes* is certainly one of the very oldest of fishes. "Bony fish" covers nearly all fish that have a bony skeleton. This differentiates them from all boneless fish, such as sharks, skates, and rays, which have only cartilaginous or gristly structures.

Eating Bonefish

Are bonefish edible?

This controversial subject has been known to lead to violence. Many natives who live in bonefish areas prize this fish as a dainty morsel. All I can personally say is that if the bonefish is "stretched" properly to remove the tiny bones, baked whole and served with a stuffing mixed with onions, peppers, and spices, then covered with a generous helping of tasty sauce, the result is an edible dish, not because it's a bonefish, but in spite of it. I wish that bonefish were even less edible, so that they would not be used for food, and instead, would be released to delight the growing number of anglers who are spending thousands of dollars in their pursuit. In many localities bonefish are netted, an easy task as they often travel in large schools and can be stampeded into a net spread across a channel or between clumps of mangroves. Furthermore, bonefish are considered the best bait for marlin, so the smaller bonefish, 2½ to 3½ pounds, are in great demand by deep-sea anglers. The current price is a dollar per fish; and thousands are netted, frozen, and sold for this purpose. Fortunately there is a growing awareness of the value of bonefish as a revenue-producing sport fish.

I know of two small communities in the Bahamas of about equal size and only 15 miles apart. One community has prohibited by law the taking of bonefish by netting; the other community still nets them. In the past ten years, the first community has had no bonefish-population decrease and a large increase in the population of tourists and winter residents, while in the other community, the bonefish have practically disappeared, with, of course, adverse effects on the tourist trade.

More and more enlightened sportsmen and their guides are releasing bonefish, especially the smaller ones. This is hard for some guides, as their friends and relatives cannot understand the releasing of fish which are so highly prized as food. Even Bonefish Joe will frequently remark rather wistfully as a three-pounder is returned to the water that it is "jes' 'bout the right size for frying."

I have personally had only two experiences in eating bonefish. The first was some years ago when I had a 2½-pound fish fried, as one would fry any fish of similar size. The results were not very good. The meat, which was snow-white and quite dry, seemed a cross between cotton and sawdust in texture and flavor. I won't dwell on the bones, which are very small and quite formidable. They kept turning up between my teeth for many days following the repast.

It was some years later that I had another try at eating bonefish, and I must admit the results were much happier. The subject of bonefish as a food fish had arisen with a lady of my acquaintance who prided herself on her small dinner parties and who had something of a reputation as a connoisseur of fine food. I had remarked on my experience with fried bonefish, and she immediately took issue with me. "You don't know what you're talking about," she exclaimed heatedly. "Why, you didn't even 'stretch' it, and who ever heard of frying a bonefish!" I didn't pursue the argument but she did and concluded by saying that if I could produce a 5-pound, or over, bonefish she would give a party on it and I would change my tune. I accepted the challenge with good grace, albeit skeptically.

Lady luck works in devious ways, and the next day on a nearby flat I brought in one that weighed slightly over 6 pounds. This I sent to my friend with a facetious note and the comment that except for her I would have been tempted to release such a noble fish. An invitation to dine the following Saturday night came a day or so later. My wife and I accepted of course. We arrived and after suitable libation, accompanied by hors d'oeuvres of conch fritters, heart of palm, and cuda (raw, chopped barracuda and onions, marinated in vinegar and used as a spread), we found ourselves seated with six others, gazing at the remains of my 6-pound bonefish. "Now," my hostess said proudly, "you're going to have bonefish as it should be served."

"Has it been properly 'stretched'?" I asked, cautiously, without the slightest idea of what stretching meant.

"Oh yes," she assured me, "that's the way we get rid of the bones. You see, the skeleton of a bonefish differs from most other fishes in that its ribs are in tiers of three instead of two and by pulling the fish lengthwise in a certain manner these bones are dislodged so that most of them can be removed after cooking."

I glanced at the fish in order to determine in what respect its shape had been altered and was unable to detect the head from the tail. "If you do not fry bonefish, just how do you cook them?" I asked.

"Baked," she said, "and stuffed."

I accepted a liberal portion of the stuffing and fish, surrounded by various tropical fruits and covered by a delicious sauce. Then came the white wine.

I must admit that baked, stuffed, and stretched bonefish was superb and produced no ill effects. But if I had not been told, I would not have known it was fish. The good lady must have worked most of the day to produce the excellent fish. And while I thoroughly enjoyed the experience I have not had a stretched bonefish since.

In all fairness to the edibility of bonefish it is probable that I am in the minority on the subject. In Japan and also in Hawaii bonefish (called 'o'io) are netted in large quantities and are highly prized as food fish. In Hawaii alone over 300,000 pounds are caught yearly and sold at prices ranging from 27 to 45 cents a pound. In both Japan and Hawaii the favorite way to prepare them is in fish cakes, and while I have not tasted the dish, its recipe is printed here for the adventurous.

FISH CAKE MADE WITH 'O'IO

Clean fish; cover and age in refrigerator for about 24 hours. Fillet fish; scrape the meat off the bones and skin with a spoon. The flesh is easily removed by scraping toward the tail of the fish. Place the flesh in a mixing bowl and then either knead the flesh with your hand or beat with an electric beater. While kneading or beating the boned flesh, slowly add salt water (1 teaspoon of salt to 1 cup water) and pepper. When mixture reaches a spongy consistency it can be seasoned with chopped green onions. Shape into patties and fry.

I have heard it said that the appeal of bonefish is not derived entirely from the palate but that an occasional bonefish in the diet will sharpen one's wits and make for cleverness and shrewdness. This is undoubtedly suggested by certain characteristics of bonefish which have given rise to the name *Albula vulpes,* or "white fox."

There is no question as to its whiteness, like a flash of silver in the sun, and I am satisfied that no other fish is endowed with such keen senses. Take eyesight, for instance. Time and again I have witnessed a bonefish spot a moving lure 20 or even 25 feet away when the water is brilliant and clear, as it usually is on tropic flats.

There is no question as to its highly developed sense of smell. Years ago, when still-fishing and chumming were in vogue on the Florida flats, I saw schools of bonefish, slowly feeding against the tide, suddenly get a scent of the chum, and rush headlong 50 or 75 feet to the waiting baits.

As to hearing, anyone who has fished the flats for bonefish knows that the slightest sound of pole against boat or a touch of the boat bottom against coral or sand hummock will flush a school of bonefish, sending them in every direction. And who has not cast to bonefish only to have one of the school brush against the monofilament line or leader? It is incredible how the alarm of that one fish will spook the entire school.

As to the fifth sense—taste—I have no evidence that one exists, and yet they certainly prefer some types of food, like crabs, to others, like conch. Whether this is a matter of eyesight or smell I do not know.

That these senses are well developed in bonefish is not hard to understand when one considers that they live in constant fear. Their feeding grounds are patrolled by sharks on the lookout for bonefish off their guard. As motionless as sunken logs, barracuda lie in wait on the flats, marking time till the unwary bonefish come within range. The quick lunge is usually to no avail for lurking barricuda—but not always. Small wonder the fate of bonefish in the survival of the fittest lies in its ability to outwit those predators who are constantly seeking to feed on it.

Highly developed senses may be one of the reasons why bonefish are in demand as a food fish in some parts of the world. Among superstitious peoples it is believed that the desirable qualities of certain animals can be acquired by eating them.

There is still some cannibalism among tribal primitives in the South Pacific, remote sections of Africa, and South America; natives believe that by eating an enemy, especially his heart, one may derive great courage and ferocity in combat.

Eating certain species of shark is supposed to endow one with great virility. The horn of rhinoceros is in great demand in India as an aphrodisiac. I have seen carcasses of rhinos in Tanganyika that were shot or trapped and from which only the horn was taken for sale. It is, of course, not really a horn at all but hair so tightly compressed as to develop sufficient strength to penetrate the steel shell of an automobile or truck.

Thus I leave you with the issue of the edibility of bonefish still unresolved. I can only suggest that when the opportunity presents itself, try a baked bonefish for yourself. But be sure it's "stretched."

If I Had Only...

Many years have passed since I was five years old
and caught my first smallmouth bass with an angle
worm impaled on a bent pin. During that long inter-
val I have used almost every type of lure which the
inventive genius of man has concocted to catch fish.
Of this formidable array of spinners, plugs, wobblers,
flies, jigs, etc., ad infinitum, perhaps 20 percent really
do the job and catch fish. The other 80 percent catch
the fishermen. Over the years my outlay in cash for
fishing in various parts of the world has been sub-

stantial. I would not want to know the total, but whatever it might be I regard it as perhaps my wisest and most rewarding investment. The dividends I have derived from this diversion have sustained me in countless ways; they have beguiled me into traveling the four corners of the earth and indeed around the world itself. The memories that derive from these activities are manifold. I think of friendships formed in many lands, of trips to faraway places with strange names, of experiences shared with others.

And most of all, memories of the big fish that got away and of those that yielded up the battle.

I recall as a lad of twelve fishing for sea trout on the St. Mary's River in Nova Scotia, my rod a dilapidated split bamboo discarded by one of my older brothers and fitted with a beatup reel with perhaps 30 or 35 yards of old silk line. Suddenly, an Atlantic salmon of perhaps 10 or 12 pounds seized my no. 10 brown hackle and to my utter astonishment and the amazement of my companions tore off all my line and with a magnificent terminal leap kept on going down river. If I had only . . .

And then there was the Pacific sailfish on the west Coast of Mexico. He smashed at the "teaser" (a sort of hookless plug trolled about 30 feet behind the launch). It served as a signal to release 20 or 30 feet of line, so that the sailfish could see the mackerel bait and have time to swallow it. Alas, I struck too soon—the great fish leaped three times in rapid succession, threw the bait, and disappeared in a flurry of spray. If I had only . . .

And then the 14-pound bonefish (estimated by Bonefish Joe) rushed off 150 yards of 8-pound-test monofilament line. The bottom was clear white sand; there were no mangroves to worry about, no coral heads to cut the line. In fact there was no trouble visible anywhere, and so I didn't stand up on the seat and hold the rod high aloft to keep my fish's chin up. Alas, I didn't see the dark shadow beneath the surface. There was an extra tug on the line, then a dead weight. When the skiff reached the spot there was a submerged sponge on the bottom with the line wrapped around it, cut by some sharp growth on the sponge surface. The fish was gone. If I had only . . .

And then on the St. Lawrence a fighting muskie on light bass tackle had battled me for almost half an hour. He was all in with tail showing, a sign of surrender, as he came to the boat with all fight gone. But I had no gaff, and the net was too small. At the very moment of victory the muskie summoned a final convulsive flurry, smashed against the side of the boat, which broke the line, and slowly struggled down into the deep water below. If I had only . . .

But these and many other battles with fish are not fought in vain. Often in the small hours of morning, when sleep eludes me, I live them over again, but with one difference—they always have a happy ending, and with it comes sleep. This is much more effective for me than counting sheep or even one's blessings, as recommended by Eisenhower. I sleep and dream that these fish did not get away after all, that I really had followed that leaping salmon down along the shore before he reached the end of the line; that I delayed striking the Pacific sailfish, giving him a few seconds to swallow the bait; that I kept the bonefish's chin up to prevent him from reaching the shadowy submerged sponge; and that I beached the fighting muskie instead of trying to land him by hand.

At this point there is a merry whistle coming down the little street of my tropical hideaway, and when it gets to my window I hear Bonefish Joe saying, "Man, we got a good mornin' comin' up. The sun is bright, the wind is jes' right, and the tide is at the low flood. Those flats will be loaded. Bring yo' fly rod."

But not all fishing trips are successful. I remember one for big trout in northern Quebec—early June— snow, sleet, and gales—a sick Indian guide—few fish and no leviathans.

Bad experiences are rare. They fade and do not seem so vivid as years pass by. I do not put fishless days in this category at all. Some of my most rewarding experiences happened on fishless days. How can one evaluate the spiritual refreshment which comes from a day alone on some lovely stream in May? To sit beside a tumbling brook when birds are nesting nearby and listen to the voice of nature will go a long way toward solving the problems that seemed so baffling in the city a few days earlier. And I know of no more absorbing adventure than to wade slowly across some white tropic flat. Although the bonefisherman may go home empty-handed, if he has eyes to see and ears to hear he will be a silent observer of the myriads of sea creatures living out their destinies all about him. He will see small sharks cruising about in the warm shallow water; aquatic plants and small fans will wave to him as the tide flows or ebbs; shells both large and small will be his audience; and birds of many species will stalk the shallows with him or fly past to join others on some coral point nearby. It is never lonely on a tropical flat, and it doesn't matter greatly whether the bonefish are biting or not that day—there are other compensations.

And it doesn't matter whether it's a tropical flat, a mountain stream, or a quiet lake. Fishing is a cleansing experience, and I can't express it better than a fellow member of the Anglers' Club, Francis Hatch, who wrote:

Fishing is not alone the intelligent pursuit of shadowy creatures beneath the surface of still or hurrying waters.

Fishing is the discovery of pale pink arbutus flowering in the shelter of an oak leaf. It is the flaming candelabra of a cardinal flower standing erect in a shadowed brook; the fragrance of a wild strawberry; or the shy beauty of a wild rose blooming in the root loop of a weatherbeaten stump.

Fishing is a pipe enjoyed, back against rock, listening to liquid love poured out on the dampening air of the evening by a hermit thrush, unseen.

Fishing is a drink which any wise physician would prescribe at the end of the day, the perfect antidote, second only to sleep, for weariness. And if perchance a clumsy boot has filled to brim with water, a drink indeed holds power to save a life.

Fishing is companionship with a company of men, each of whom, along the stream or around the fire, divesting himself of all disruptions of the world, reverts to the simple man, welcomed and respected by others who are similarly blessed with the power to comprehend.

APPENDIX:
Concise Guide to Bonefishing

SCIENTIFIC NAME
Albula vulpes

COMMON NAMES
Bonefish, banana fish, Macabi macaco,   'o'io, grubber

DISTRIBUTION
The shallows of all tropic and warm semitropic seas.

TACKLE FOR BOAT FISHING
3/6 split bamboo or glass rod. 1/0 or 2/0 multiple action reel
with star drag with 200 yards of 20-pound-test nylon or Da-
cron monofilament line. 4/0 hook and 1-ounce sinker.

SPINNING
6½- or 7-foot split-bamboo or glass two-piece rod—5- to 7-
ounce weight—slow action. Spinning reel with capacity of
300 yards of monofilament line, 6- to 10-pound-test (8-pound
preferred by author).
NOTE. 300 yards will permit loss of up to 100 yards of line,
and most spinning reels for bonefishing will accommodate
this much line.

FLY ROD

9- or 9½-foot split-bamboo or glass rod with medium action. Reel capable of holding 200 yards of backing plus casting line and with adjustable drag but no click. This matter of click is debatable. Some bonefishermen feel that the pleasure of a screaming reel outweighs the possible spooking of a fish as the noise vibrations descend the line and enter the water. A No. 20 Walker reel has a variable drag and an optional click which can be used on or off. A very popular but expensive reel, it has either single or multiple action.

A tapered nylon line or line with torpedo head and 6- to 9-foot leader of nylon from a heavy butt section to 8- or 10-pound-test tippet.

LURES

For bait fishing: Crabs of all kinds, crawfish, shrimp, conch, or clams.

For spinning: Use these same baits or weighted flies (1/9-ounce preferred), wiggle jigs, spinners, and miscellaneous spinning lures.

For fly rod: Use any type illustrated earlier in this book. Size of hook 1/0 to no. 6 long shank. Streamers of the breather type and large bucktails are good. White, yellow, and black are preferred colors, and some tinsel in the bodies is very good. A pink shrimp fly is quite effective and also a bucktail made by Wm. Mills and Son called the Mills.

BOAT

12- to 16-foot skiff with flat or nearly flat bottom—plywood or wood are better than aluminum or plastic as they are less noisy and more stable in the wind. Outboard motor, an oar, and 10-foot pole with blunt end or rubber shoe (not metal) to eliminate noise against the bottom. The boat should have a wide seat or platform in the bow for the angler to stand on.

GLASSES

Best-grade polaroid glasses are essential.

SHOES

It is important to use shoes which will not slip on a wet boat bottom. They should have rubber soles for quietness.

HEAD COVERING

A hat which will protect neck and ears and with a large peak is important. Blond anglers and those particularly susceptible to sunburn, especially of the lips, should have plenty of effective lotion. A surgeon's mask is 100 percent effective and in time it's easy to get used to it. I use one with holes cut in the nose section for easy breathing.

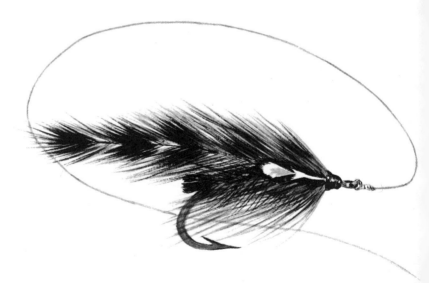

INDEX